DEVELOPING YOUR THEORETICAL ORIENTATION IN COUNSELING AND PSYCHOTHERAPY

DEVELOPING YOUR THEORETICAL ORIENTATION IN COUNSELING AND PSYCHOTHERAPY

DUANE HALBUR

University of North Dakota

KIMBERLY VESS HALBUR

North Dakota State University

Boston ■ New York ■ San Francisco
Mexico City ■ Montreal ■ Toronto ■ London ■ Madrid ■ Munich ■ Paris
Hong Kong ■ Singapore ■ Tokyo ■ Cape Town ■ Sydney

Executive Editor: *Virginia Lanigan*
Series Editorial Assistant: *Scott Blaszak*
Marketing Manager: *Kris Ellis-Levy*
Editorial Production Service: *Barbara Gracia*
Composition and Manufacturing Buyer: *Andrew Turso*
Electronic Composition: *Publishers' Design and Production Services, Inc.*
Cover Administrator: *Rebecca Krzyzaniak*

For related titles and support materials, visit our online catalog at www.ablongman.com.

Between the time website information is gathered and then published, it is not unusual for some sites to have closed. Also, the transcription of URLs can result in typographical errors. The publisher would appreciate notification where these occur so that they may be corrected in subsequent editions.

Library of Congress Cataloging-in-Publication Data

Halbur, Duane.
    Developing your theoretical orientation in counseling and psychotherapy / Duane Halbur, Kimberly Vess Halbur.
        p. cm.
    Includes bibliographical references and index.
    ISBN 0-205-39677-1
        1. Psychology—Philosophy. 2. Counseling. 3. Psychotherapy. I. Halbur, Kimberly Vess. II. Title

BF38.H33 2006
158'.3—dc22   2005050995

Printed in the United States of America

10 9 8 7 6 5 4 3 2 1   09 08 07 06 05

In memory of
Edna May Thompson
and
Carol Lynn Halbur
who gave us much love and many of our theories about life

CONTENTS

■ ■ ■ ■ ■

CHAPTER THREE
Top Ten Ways to Find Your Theoretical Orientation   21

CHAPTER FOUR
Five Schools of Thought and Their Theories of Helping   39

PREFACE

We wrote *Developing Your Theoretical Orientation* with the objective of assisting other helping professionals find their theoretical orientation more easily than we did. We realize that *helping professionals* may seem like a generic term, however, we use it in an effort to include helpers who work with diverse populations in a wide array of fields. Specifically, we are speaking to mental health counselors, psychologists, social workers, school counselors, substance abuse counselors, psychotherapists, and peer helpers. We sincerely hope that this text will assist helpers in each of these disciplines find and solidify their theoretical orientation.

Because the work of helping professionals needs to be grounded in theory, we have featured in this book an innovative model for selecting a theoretical orientation and hands-on activities to assist students in their quest for a theoretical approach to helping. The Intentional Theory Selection (ITS) model is a contemporary model for selecting a theoretical orientation. This model can assist helpers in finding a theory that is congruent with their personal values. We also acknowledge that the selection of a theoretical orientation may be quite cyclical. Just as in life, change in theoretical orientation is constant and inevitable. Thus, a professional helper may revisit the model many times throughout his or her career.

In Chapter 2, the Intentional Theory Selection (ITS) model is first presented conceptually and described more thoroughly. Chapter 3 presents the top ten ways for helpers to find their theoretical orientation. Chapter 4 serves as a primer of the helping theories. Finally in Chapter 5, students, clinicians, and supervisors share their experiences in applying the model in training and clinical practice. These cases illuminate for the reader how to use the model. They also provide the reader with the opportunity to see that many of the professional helper's challenges are universal. We hope that these applied examples will assist helpers to understand not just that theory is central to the helping professional but also how to integrate theory and make it personal and meaningful in their professional work.

This book may also serve as a reminder or overview of the foremost helping theories and their respective schools of thought. As presented, we provide the reader with a reminder of the basic philosophies, goals, and techniques of the major theories of counseling. We hope this book offers just enough information to remind professional helpers of what they already know, while enticing them to seek out and learn more about a presented theory.

In addition to a summary of selected counseling theories, students will be exposed to ten applied ways to aid in the self-discovery process. This self-discovery will begin the students' process of intentionally finding a theoretical orientation that is congruent with their own worldview, beliefs, and values. The Selective Theoretical Sorter (STS) is a survey that was developed to help students discover which researched theories they might endorse. This sorter, more important in self-discovery than in assessment, is one of several tools students will be offered in the process of finding their own theoretical orientation.

We hope that readers find the material and the ITS model refreshing and at the same time meaningful. Those in the helping-professions field know through research and observation that theory is important. Additionally, many innovators, researchers, and clinicians have dedicated their research and life work to finding techniques and philosophies that can best serve our clientele. We owe so much to these pioneers who have helped us to be effective and ethical in the work we do.

The helping fields are truly important to a developing society. Helping professionals have the opportunity to prevent and remediate when they serve in a field that makes its daily impact by improving the individual lives of others. As you work on your own professional identity and struggles, remember that this opportunity is both a blessing and a responsibility. In this book, as in many endeavors in your professional life, you will be asked to look inward. As professionals, we ask this of clients, as authors we ask this of you. Take this opportunity to challenge yourself and grow.

We have presented the Intentional Theory Selection (ITS) model and the Selective Theory Sorter (STS) at several professional conferences and have greatly appreciated the feedback and the anticipation for this project to be in print. We still receive emails and phone calls asking for the information that we now have on paper. The interest we have received professionally has served as a muse and motivation for us to write.

Additionally, we have been fortunate to have interest and support for this text from a wonderful group of colleagues. Their help and support for this project have been invaluable to us. We would like to thank those professionals who gave us permission to incorporate their learning experiences with our model in this text. We are so appreciative of the efforts of Kristin Schloemer, Jim Wilwerding, Jen Olsen, Ryan Flaherty, Jamie Glenn-Burns, Shannon Beelner, and Krista Strauser as well as our faithful research assistant Robert Johnson. We would also like to thank the following people for reviewing this book:

Alfiee M. Breland, Michigan State University
Michael J. Bologna, College of Saint Rose
Lisa K. Comer, University of Northern Colorado
Mary H. Duggan, Old Dominion University
Jeannine Feldman, San Diego State University
Ron Jacques, Brigham Young University, Idaho
Kristi Kanel, California State University, Fullerton
Leslie A. Moore, University of Texas at Austin

Each of them provided feedback and suggestions that were crucial to the development of this book.

DEVELOPING YOUR THEORETICAL ORIENTATION IN COUNSELING AND PSYCHOTHERAPY

CHAPTER ONE

WHY THEORETICAL ORIENTATION IS IMPORTANT

It is impossible for a man to learn what he thinks he already knows.
—Epictetus

A PERSONAL EXPERIENCE

Since our first years of teaching graduate counseling classes, students have often asked, "How did you decide your theoretical orientation?" This question is reasonable and understandable, because students in the helping professions are frequently asked about their theoretical orientation. Thus, we began pondering the development of our own theoretical orientations, that inevitably centered around three core issues: personalities, mentors and supervisors, and clients.

First, we contemplated how personality might play a role in the theories that we liked and the ways we worked with clients. For example, one of us is an outgoing, energetic person who reflects these traits in interactions with others, both personally and professionally, and who sets high standards and believes that, in general, people strive to do what they believe is right. The other, however, tends to focus on philosophical understanding and consequently, practices Socratic questioning in everyday life. These personal tendencies greatly influence our theories. For example, one focuses on social and humanistic theories, while the other works with theories that have strong philosophical foundations. Personal qualities, values, actions, and assumptions clearly impact our theoretical orientations and, consequently, our work with clients.

Next, we thought about our mentors and supervisors and the various theoretical orientations they espoused. For instance one mentor was very clearly humanistic and relied on gestalt interventions. Some faculty members were fairly diverse in their theoretical orientations, and championed constructivist, client-centered, cognitive-behavioral, and ecological approaches. One clinical supervisor said he was a "planned eclectic." These mentors and supervisors greatly impacted our choices of theoretical orientation. Their feedback, guidance, and expectations were always tinted because of their theoretical orientation. As a result, we knew that they had impacted our choices as well. We were just not sure how.

Acknowledging that we had been exposed to a wealth of theoretical orientations, we began to think about past and present clients with whom we had worked. We thought about how effective our theoretical orientations were for them. We concluded that each client must have also impacted us as we selected our theoretical orientations. Despite, or perhaps because of, our examinations of these theoretical-orientation issues, we seemed to answer students by saying, *"You just figure it out as you go along. When a theory really 'fits' for you, you will know it."*

Fortunately, we knew this answer was not satisfactory. We remembered all too well our first years as helping professionals. We had often been quizzed about our own theoretical orientations, and yet we had not been given any tools other than the required survey course in major theories to help us. As we recounted our own similar struggles, we realized how very important theoretical orientation is in the helping professions. Thus, we wanted to offer our students specific strategies to use in developing their theoretical orientation.

THE BIG PUZZLE

Selecting a theoretical orientation is typically a puzzling experience for students in the helping professions. A common goal of training programs is to teach effective helping skills. Academic programs also strive to help students conduct counseling in a way that is intentional and theory based. Consequently, students are frequently asked during the course of their graduate programs to state their theoretical orientation, typically by writing a paper about it. The assignment usually goes something like this: After reading a brief overview of counseling theories, which one do you believe fits your style of counseling?

Although this assignment is valuable, it may occur too early in the education of professional helpers. Because these students do not yet have enough clinical experience to guide them, they typically respond to the theoretical-orientation assignment by picking theories that sound good on paper. Students, at this stage usually, have little understanding of the theories they choose. Unfortunately, many students continue to support, research, and apply their chosen theory, which ultimately limits their overall understanding of counseling theories. Some students simply choose the instructor's theoretical orientation in hope of receiving a high grade on the assignment. Others pick the theory that they best understood. It is not that students are attempting to be lazy or manipulate instructors for a higher grade, rather, they are overwhelmed by the multitude of theories and therapeutic interventions to which they are exposed. Even when students find theories that they like on paper, they often feel lost and unable to apply theory to practice. Hence, most students in the helping professions find it extremely difficult to develop and articulate in both words and practice their own theoretical orientation. This dilemma can easily be compared to the experience of holding pieces to a jigsaw puzzle without having the picture on the front of the box. On the journey to finding a theoretical orientation, the role of soul-searching and clinical practice cannot be emphasized enough. Although this book does not offer clinical experience, it does provide for self-evaluation and soul-searching. Through the use of applied methods, the Intentional Theory Selection (ITS) model, case studies, and the Selective Theory Sorter (STS), counselors in training may begin to complete a puzzle that culminates in forming their theoretical orientation.

WHAT IS THEORETICAL ORIENTATION?

Before students in the helping professions can begin the voyage to finding and solidi-fying a theoretical orientation, they must first have a working definition of the term *theoretical orientation*. This definition enables students, counselors, and the field in general to have a similar idea of what being theoretically orientated means. Poznanski and McLennan (1995) provide an excellent definition: a theoretical orientation is "a conceptual framework used by a counselor to understand client therapeutic needs" (p. 412). More specifically, theoretical orientation provides helpers with a theory-based framework for "(a) generating hypotheses about a client's experience and behavior, (b) formulating a rationale for specific treatment interventions, and (c) evaluating the on-going therapeutic process" (Poznanski & McLennan, 1995, p. 412). Thus, theoretical orientation forms the foundation for helping professionals in counseling, social work, and applied psychology. Having a theoretical orientation provides helpers with goals and techniques that set the stage for translating theory into practice (Strupp, 1955).

As students in the helping professions learn skills and theories, they often struggle with ways to integrate the information. For example, in counseling classes students may learn to express empathy and to confront, but they do not yet understand how to practice those skills with the intention that follows a specific, theoretical orientation. By choosing a theoretical orientation to practice and applying it, a counselor is able to use general counseling skills in an applied and intentional way.

THE HELPER'S TOOL BELT

Once counselors learn the basic helping skills, they then have the opportunity to use them in an intentional way. In many ways a theoretical orientation serves as a tool belt. The tool belt is filled with a multitude of different tools that serve different functions. Among the tools counselors will find the basic skills of confrontation, reflection of feeling, open-ended questions, and empathy. Additionally, counselors who have a theoretical foundation have tools specific to their theory. For example, a Gestalt counselor has the tool of the *empty-chair technique*, and the behaviorist counselor has the tool of *behavioral contracting*. Any of these tools can be useful in the construction (helping) process. All of the techniques have the potential of achieving the same desired result: helping the client.

For example, a student enrolled in a graduate counseling program is seeing a client at his practicum site. The client, a college freshman, is very frustrated with her mother and anxious about going home over the holiday break. The student believes that the client needs to express her feelings toward her mother. Depending on the counselor's theoretical orientation, the tool selected for the expression of the client's feelings may vary. If the counselor ascribes to rational emotive behavioral therapy (REBT), he may explore with the client her irrational beliefs about going home for the holidays. Or, if the counselor works from an existential framework, he might encourage the client to be authentic with her mother regarding her feelings of frustration. However, if the counselor ascribes to Gestalt theory, he may decide to use the empty-chair technique promoting the client to express her feelings during the session. In this particular case, the counselor decided to use the empty-chair technique. The intervention looked somewhat awkward and the counselor was clearly uncomfortably with the intervention and the processing of it with his client. After the session, the counselor said to his instructor; "Wasn't that awful? I can't believe it didn't work. I really thought the client would like it." Unfortunately, the counselor picked an intervention that really was not in his typical tool belt because his stated theory was REBT. He used an intervention, a tool, which was not congruent with his theory. Although using a wrench to pound a nail can be done, it will likely not feel right and may not be as effective.

WHAT CAN A THEORETICAL ORIENTATION DO FOR ME?

A theoretical orientation provides helpers with a framework for therapy that sets the foundation for intentional counseling. For the counselor, being intentional is a prerequisite to ethical and effective helping. Theory is an important factor in structuring therapy and directing interventions (Hansen & Freimuth, 1997). Consequently, intentional counseling requires counselors to rely on their theoretical orientation to guide therapy. Thus, when counselors get lost in the therapeutic process, theory can provide a roadmap. Theory is also a way for counselors to organize and listen to data and information given to them by clients. A number of theories provide specific steps to treatment planning; these steps may assist counselors in being intentional and consistent in their role as a therapist. Ideally, counselors' interventions would stem from their theoretical orientation, however, human beings do not fit neatly into categories. As Hackney (1992), who has eloquently written about theory and process, states, like human nature, "client problems are typically multidimensional" (p. 2). The following is a clinical example.

Louis, a 23-year-old, Mexican American male seeks therapy. During the initial interview, he states: "I am a loser. I have a college degree and can't get a job. I don't ask people out on dates because I know they'll see immediately that I'm a loser. When I do go out to meet people, women seem to avoid me." The therapist believes the client has a problem with self-esteem. While self-esteem is an important facet of the client's experience, self-esteem needs to be viewed from a larger perspective. The client's problem seems to encompass his thinking, feeling, behavior, and interactions with the world around him. A therapist who has a specific theoretical orientation will be able to view the client holistically knowing that the theory will provide a roadmap for the therapy.

Espousing a theoretical orientation to helping has numerous benefits for both clinicians and the clients they serve. Specifically, a theoretical orientation provides ways to organize client information. An orientation can also help intentionality and consistency within the work of a professional helper. Although the helper should understand what a theoretical orientation is, why it is important, and what it can do for both client and counselor, this information provides little help to a counselor who must pick a theory from which to work. The ways in which others have picked a theory may help students understand where they can go to secure a working theory.

HOW HAVE OTHERS PICKED A
THEORETICAL ORIENTATION?

Most helpers choose their theoretical orientation based on one of three considerations: (1) the theoretical orientation of the helper's training program, (2) the helper's life philosophy, and/or (3) the helper's professional experience and/or a client (Hackney, 1992). While these traditional methods are common ways that helpers find their theoretical orientation, each has inherent pitfalls. The shortcomings of each of these methods will be discussed in order to provide a rationale for a new model of choosing a theory that is presented in Chapter 2.

First, initial training programs may or may not expose students to every theoretical orientation. For example, if faculty members at the same institution support the same theoretical orientation, they limit their students' exposure to the myriad of available theories. Conversely, if students enroll in an academic program where every faculty member has a different theoretical orientation, the students may receive mixed messages about "effective" therapy. Another potential difficulty for students is underexposure to the *process* of developing a personal orientation, because faculties choose not to discuss their own theoretical orientation in hopes of being unbiased in their teaching. Thus, a theoretical orientation to helping cannot be based solely on students' training programs.

Second, some counselors base their theoretical orientation on their own personality and philosophy of life. This approach can also present difficulties. For example, counselors who are predominantly optimistic and believe in the best in people may choose a humanistic approach. Other counselors may believe that peoples' thoughts are the core of their problems and choose rational emotive behavior therapy (REBT) as a way to help clients develop more rational thinking. Both beliefs ultimately influence how counselors perceive, interact with, and treat their clients, even if those clients may have a personality and worldview much different from the counselors. Although theory provides a framework for working with most clients, counselors must remember that each client is unique. A counselor must remain both open to experience and flexible with clients.

The third way helpers determine their theoretical orientation is through clinical experience, even though helpers may realize that their theoretical orientation does not fit for all clients or clinical situations. For example, counselors who favor a humanistic orientation may have difficulty in career-counseling settings. While these counselors may be skilled at reflection of feeling, genuineness, and rapport building that lay at the core of the humanistic approach, their clients who are seeking resume reviews and job information may feel frustrated when they get a "listening ear" but not the results they expected, such as direct advice on finding an internship or tips on interviewing. In such cases, counselors need to adjust their theory to fit the needs of the client. Counselors must maintain their fundamental beliefs and values regarding the helping relationship but must also adapt their interventions so as to help the client. In this example, a humanist in a career-counseling situation may choose to hold onto the belief that people are basically good and striving for actualization. However, in an attempt to meet the needs of the client, the humanistic career counselor may be open to a change of perception—one that acknowledges that formal career exploration can lead to greater actualization. In another example, while attempting to be grounded in theory, a cognitive-behavioral therapist utilized cognitive techniques that were not appropriate for her client, because the client had low-intellectual functioning. In attempting to stay completely in harmony with her theory, the therapist was not meeting her client's needs. Consequently, she had to adapt her style and take a more behavioral approach.

Over the course of a therapist's career, existing theories will be revised, and new theories will evolve. Through continued learning and openness to emerging ideas, counselors can avoid becoming stagnant in a constantly changing field.

ONCE I HAVE IT, HOW CAN I USE IT?

Once a counselor's theoretical orientation is developed, it must be put into action. Theoretical orientation is used as a blueprint to organize a client's information as well as a tool to guide clinical decisions, diagnosis, intervention selection, and treatment planning. Theoretical orientation can help determine the direction and activities used during the course of counseling. Certainly, counselors use theory to explain or conceptualize clients' problems. According to Kottler (1999), theory is "the place to start when you are trying to sort out a complex, confusing situation" (p. 30). Similarly, Strohmer, Shivy, and Chodo (1990) suggest that counselors may also use theoretical orientation to selectively confirm their hypotheses regarding their clients. Not only does theoretical orientation help in case conceptualization, diagnosis, and treatment planning, it may also allow for a clinician to behave ethically.

HOW ARE THEORETICAL ORIENTATION AND ETHICS RELATED?

Clinicians are ethically and often legally bound to have a theoretical foundation. Informed consent is a component of many professional ethical codes such as those of the American Counseling Association (ACA), the American Psychological Association (APA), and the National Association of Social Workers (NASW). Each of these professional ethics codes provides that clients enter the helping relationship with informed consent. Implicit within the notion of informed consent is that helpers should share their theoretical orientation with clients and must at least be able to articulate their theory if asked by clients. Helpers who share their theoretical orientation with clients allow them to make an informed choice to engage in therapy. Thus, helpers need to be able to articulate their theoretical orientation and how it impacts the helping relationship and the therapeutic process. Additionally, many states dictate that licensed practitioners provide their clients with a professional disclosure statement. Such a statement usually orients the client to the counseling process and typically includes information about the helper's educational background and areas of expertise, length of sessions, responsibilities of each party, hourly fee, and the helper's theoretical orientation. Thus, helpers need to be able to articulate their theoretical orientation in order to behave ethically and professionally.

HOW CAN THEORETICAL ORIENTATION HELP YOU EXAMINE VALUES?

Another aspect of ethical behavior involves the examination of both the counselor's and client's values. Having a theoretical orientation allows clinicians to effectively incorporate values into the counseling process (Consoli & Williams, 1999; Mahalik, 1995). Several studies indicated that counselors as a whole possess a shared culture characterized by similar values that go beyond one's typical orientation (Consoli & Williams, 1999).

Within the shared professional culture, several specific values exist. In general, counselors embrace the personal values of benevolence, self-direction, universalism, and achievement but devalue power and tradition (Kelly, 1995). Counselors also endorse the mental health values of autonomy, purposeful personal development, responsible self-expression, compassionate responsiveness, positive human relatedness, sexual acceptance, and forgiveness. One study focused on clinicians with distinct theoretical orientations (cognitive-behavioral, existential or person-centered, psychoanalytic, and family systems) and surveyed these practitioners about their values (Mahalik, 1995). Counselors as a group showed consensus in the values they endorsed despite their divergent theoretical orientations. In this study, counselors specifically valued individualism and autonomy, emphasized emotional spontaneity and self-expression over self-control, and endorsed harmony with nature over mastery or submission.

Thus, the research appears to show that counselors have a shared, but not unanimous, professional culture. Specifically, counselors tend to value personal development and achievement that involve others in a significant way (intimacy, loyalty, commitment). Counselors also endorse the pursuit of meaning and purpose in life, and they do so in a way that is relevant individually, interpersonally, and environmentally.

It is important to understand that counselors have a shared professional culture with its own implicit and explicit values. Consequently, counselors may struggle with clients perceived as power hungry, closed minded, racist, or not in favor of self-expression and freedom. While helpers should know that counselors and mental health practitioners share certain values that can potentially link them together and that their shared professional culture is not necessarily representative of the values and beliefs held by clients. Additionally, counselors, too, have various values and beliefs. Current research suggests a shared culture, but this research examines the majority view. The risk of losing the voice of diverse and minority counselors is real and cannot be ignored. Although various theories do make assumptions about the values of the clinician, theories exist that are congruent with most value systems. Consequently, clinicians have the opportunity to understand the values inherent in the professional culture through such avenues as research and ethical codes. However, clinicians must determine their own individual values. An important step for clinicians in determining theoretical orientation is understanding and clarifying personal values. Determining theoretical orientation is not a one-time task. Helpers should continuously examine both values and theoretical orientation as they grow, develop, and experience life changes.

THE MAIN POINTS

In summary, helping professionals must develop a theoretical orientation that gives them a blueprint for building ethical, helping relationships based on values, personality, and intention. This ongoing process will ultimately make helpers more confident and effective in serving the needs of their clients.

This textbook will assist students in developing their theoretical orientation by providing them with the opportunity for self-examination through many forms, including, the Intentional Theory Selection (ITS) model, which is presented in Chapter 2, reflection questions, specific activities such as value clarification, processing of personality type, and utilization of the Selective Theory Sorter (STS), which is presented in Chapter 3.

REFLECTION QUESTIONS

1. If you had to select your theoretical orientation today, what would it be? How confident are you with your current choice of theoretical orientation?

2. What experiences have you had with clients that either support or negate your current theoretical orientation?

3. What influences have your faculty and supervisors had on your theoretical orientation?

4. How intentional are the techniques and interventions you use with clients?

5. What values do you have that could conflict with those of a client such as prolife, belief in the sanctity of marriage, belief that physical abuse is wrong?

CHAPTER TWO

INCORPORATING THEORY INTO PRACTICE

*When one day one perceives that their occupations are . . . no longer linked with
living, why not then continue to look like a child upon it all as upon something
unfamiliar, from out of the depth of one's own world . . .*

—Rainer Maria Rilke

Practitioners and researchers alike contend that for effective and intentional counseling to occur helping professionals must adopt a comprehensive counseling theory. Theory serves as a conceptual framework and guide to interventions and assists helpers in the process of effective counseling. Consequently, being theory driven is important; yet, helpers have many theories to understand. Additionally, knowing the various theories and espousing one specific paradigm is not sufficient for helpers to translate theory into practice. Placing theory on a practical level requires more than textbook knowledge and a desire to be theory based. First, a helper must make an intentional cognitive shift. This shift, which is necessary for the most effective counseling, starts with a process of self-exploration, is built upon a foundation of knowledge, and if successful, culminates with the ability to move to client-counselor action. For the greatest therapeutic gains, helpers should begin to think in new ways. However, understanding and integrating a personal theory of counseling is often a foreign process, especially to the neophyte helper.

MAKING THEORY USEFUL: A MODEL

Making theory practical requires a process that starts with increased self-knowledge and ends with techniques to help clients. In counseling practicum courses students often ask, "Now what do I do with him?" or "What technique do you think would be best to use now?" Although quite relevant, these questions are similar to a golfer asking a caddy which clubs to use before learning the art of the golf swing. In order for you as helpers to do ethical and intentional counseling, a process of development must occur.

9

This development is not a linear process. Cognitive and personal changes will likely occur as you have new experiences and learn more about yourself and the world around you. Consequently, beginning helpers, as well as the most seasoned of professionals, will have moments where their theoretical orientation is challenged. Although difficult, when challenged, the helper must undergo intentional development to become more confident and effective.

If traveled successfully, the road to development begins with self-reflection and ends with application. Making theory practical starts first with the understanding of what we call *life philosophy*. Obviously, as your life experiences change, your view of the world will also change. Thus, your counseling theory and ultimately the techniques you use may change over the course of your career. A commonly expressed fear of many beginning counselors is that once they have adopted one theory, it will be tattooed on their foreheads for all instructors, supervisors, and future clients to judge. However, this worry is unnecessary because as helpers change so will their theory.

THEORY DEVELOPMENT

Through self-awareness, helpers may begin the ongoing and ever-evolving process of theory development. This development will continue to unfold for helping professionals as their life philosophy changes through experiences and insight. Once a counselor takes the first step of self-knowledge through experience, classes, and reading, the next step is to gain a general understanding of the five major schools of thought. The schools of thought serve almost as families of ideas, each with related yet unique members. About 250 established theories have been identified and put into families or schools of thought. These theories are often categorized together by identifying specific ideological similarities. One way to categorize theories is through the following five schools of thought: (1) *psychodynamic*, (2) *behavioral*, (3) *humanistic*, (4) *pragmatic*, and (5) *contemporary approaches*. These schools of thought hold unique philosophies regarding human nature, thus a general understanding of them is a key component in selecting a working theory. Further, each of these schools is represented by specific, finely honed theories. For example, within the pragmatic school several paramount theories exist, such as rational emotive behavioral therapy (REBT), which focuses on being rational and thinking logically. The related, yet contrasting, reality therapy focuses on taking control of one's actions and confronting the consequences (Ivey, Ivey, & Simek-Morgan, 1997). Adopting a specific theory from a school is similar to picking a blue crayon from a package of 100 crayons that has several shades and hues of blue. Hence, like the color blue, the various theories in each school have hues that are similar yet distinct.

Once clinicians examine life-philosophy, adopt a school of thought, and select a specific theory, they are ready to take some action. At this stage, helping professionals need to develop goals and techniques for therapy that are supported by their theoretical orientation. This, too, is challenging, because the uniqueness of clients will frequently require that helping professionals use different techniques like pulling tools from a tool belt.

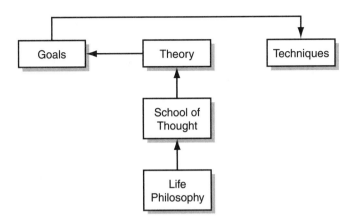

FIGURE 2.1   **Intentional Theory Selection Model**

Although the process of making theory practical may seem overwhelming now, it is manageable if students follow several steps. In the next several sections, these steps will be described. Later in the book, information, case studies, and activities are presented to help counselors gain awareness and make effective choices toward choosing and solidifying a theoretical orientation.

The Intentional Theory Selection (ITS) model of selecting a theoretical orientation is utilized as an example throughout this book (see Figure 2.1). The ITS model incorporates those aspects of theory selection that were found through research with students to be most significant in their personal solidification of theory. This model may be used not only to help students find their theoretical point of reference but also as an aid in finding an orientation that is congruent with the helping professional's individual values.

IMPORTANCE OF YOUR LIFE PHILOSOPHY

Life philosophy is the foundation of the ITS model. As a helper, being anchored in theory first requires that you have self-understanding and insight. You must become aware of how you view your world and must gain a greater comprehension of your own values (Hansen & Freimuth, 1997; Watts, 1993). Considering the questions—What is truth? Are people good? How do we gain knowledge? What causes behavior? Is spirituality important? What is right? It appears a revisit to Philosophy 101 is approaching. However, as a helper, you do not need to seek the writings of philosophers, instead you have the opportunity to be introspective. You have the opportunity to look inside of yourself and identify your own "assumptive world" (Hansen & Freimuth, 1997, p. 656). Your assumptive world is like a camera lens containing your ideas, beliefs, and values through which you perceive the world around you. Understanding how you view yourself, others, and the world around you is the first step in placing theory into a practical realm. These personal and motivating beliefs are core to your every action.

Your schema of the world is not just core to what you do, but it is ultimately the center of who you are. Helping professionals learn to help clients identify what they value and ultimately what gives meaning to their lives. As helpers incorporate theory into practice, they undergo a similar process. Once aware of your own views, you can then move to adopting a counseling theory that not only serves clients in intentional ways, but also complements who you are as a unique individual. An often-quoted phrase of Socrates, "an unexamined life is not worth living," holds true for helping professionals, as well. Without understanding your own life philosophy, you will find it harder to provide effective counseling. As teachers, we have a bias that all worthwhile endeavors in life first require self-understanding.

An additional building block of life philosophy is what you find personally meaningful. Whether this belief comes from family, ethnicity, traditions, spirituality, culture, or is created personally, it will greatly impact how you work with clients. At the root of the questions—What keeps you going? What gives you inspiration? Why do you awake each day?—is an important revelation: your purpose, your life's meaning.

Your beliefs, values, and meanings are key components to who you are and your own subjective world. Yet, you are so much more. For example, you are products of your culture, ethnicity, gender, family, orientation and religion. Your values and beliefs are founded on where you come from and where you intend to go. We recently, asked a class of ours, "What do you value?" We received the typical and expected answers—family, work, my children, friends, being honest, working hard. However, several students had immediate, overt nonverbal reactions when one international student responded, *dependence*. We asked these students to clarify their reactions, and they discussed their values of autonomy, empowerment, and independence. Their values, like their classmate's values, were greatly influenced by their cultural background and where they came from. You are influenced by your traditions and your adoption or adaptation of those traditions. Your life philosophy is indeed your own, yet, it is comprised of many influences.

As a field, the helping professions are becoming vastly more diverse as are the clients it serves. As we pointed out to our class, values, beliefs, and worldviews are not either right or wrong. It is paramount for helping professionals to identify their philosophy of life but not judge it. For example, is the student who valued dependence wrong? No. However that student must understand her value and how it may impact her theoretical orientation and her work with clients. Conversely, those students who valued independence must understand that this value is not held by everyone. They must be careful to make no assumptions about the personal worldviews of the clients they serve.

SCHOOLS OF THOUGHT

As a student, the truly difficult step in adopting a theory is gaining self-knowledge. Once you identify your own life philosophy you can begin to intentionally examine the schools of thought that drive theory. Luckily, this initial examination of theory only requires the abilities to read, listen, and comprehend. The information is available in this book and in a multitude of other resources. Beyond classroom lectures, you can find a bounty of literature describing theory and the various schools of thought. This step in the process towards adopting a theory is simply to learn. Knowing the multitude of facts surrounding each theorist, counseling history, and the specific rhetoric of each school is not a prerequisite at this stage. However, you must begin to learn the basic assumptions of each theory, which will empower you to identify those theories that seem to hold similar assumptions to your own life philosophy. Consequently, you may take on a process of discovery in which you look for those applications that are congruent with the core of who you are.

Professional helpers are not in complete agreement on how many general schools of thought exist. However, they typically count four to five (e.g., Corsini, 1979; Ivey, Ivey, & Simek-Morgan, 1997). In this book, we identify five major schools of thought: (1) psychodynamic, (2) behavioral, (3) humanistic, (4) pragmatic, and (5) contemporary approaches. Although these schools of thought may seem distinct, similarities between them will make the job of choosing one more challenging. However, these schools of thought are diverse in their assumptions regarding how personality develops, how pathology is perceived, how health is achieved, and the role of the counselor. For example, the counseling theory of existentialism within the humanistic school of thought espouses that clients' health is achieved through helping clients embrace meaning in their lives, while cognitive-behavioral approaches assist clients in developing more effective views of themselves and the world. While both approaches have proven successful in helping clients achieve more fulfilling lives, the underlying philosophies are quite different. Thus helpers must first be orientated to the basic philosophies of the major schools of thought (see Chapter 4). Choosing your school of thought is ultimately an attempt to find a "fit" for you. Some schools of thought may leave you feeling that something is missing, while other schools may leave you feeling that you have found a natural match. However, choosing a school of thought will run a smoother course after you have completed the first step of personal reflection.

THEORIES

Once you have identified your own life philosophy and have a general understanding of the school of thought that best fits your beliefs, you are then ready to pick your theory or theories. This process begins when you gain a general understanding of the various theorists within the school of thought that is most congruent to your life philosophy (Watts, 1993). For example, within the psychodynamic school do you agree with Sigmund Freud who viewed humans as mostly sexual creatures, or with Alfred Adler who saw humans primarily as social creatures? At this stage you will likely begin looking for those theories that most parallel your own views by a process of comparing and contrasting. As you pick the theory that matches most closely your own, you will begin to feel yourself gaining a stronger foundation.

In choosing your theory, you should understand that anyone can build a theory. However, the theoretical approaches that are generally published are those proven to have some generalized effectiveness (Kottler, 2002). As you move toward acceptance of a theory, you may experience times of anxiety or frustration in the process. At times you will find dissonance between your own beliefs and the theories with which you are confronted. This dissonance results in emotional consequences, which is part of a natural developmental process. Once you identify with a specific theorist, however, you are likely to have a general sense of relief as you find direction and may feel more confident in your interactions with clients (Mahoney, 1991).

Finding your theory is ultimately like finding the trunk of your helping tree. Your life philosophy serves as your soil and nutrients, feeding all that you do. Your adopted school of thought is the trunk, holding all that you do with your clients. The branches, the theories you choose, support all that you demonstrate to clients and all that you do to serve them therapeutically. Finally, these theories offer what you actually give to your clients. The leaves and fruits, your goals and techniques, provide your clients supporting shade and give them sustenance to grow. Gaining a better understanding of the schools of thought and their theories will prepare you to provide counseling and psychotherapy that is intentional (see Chapter 4).

GOALS AND TECHNIQUES: INTERVENTIONS AT WORK

After making a theoretical choice, the next step for the helper is to act. "The therapist must give advanced attention to the technique, approach, assignment, or cathartic target that will form the basis for interventions" (Jongsma & Peterson, 1995). What techniques you as a helper ultimately choose, however, will, and should, be based on your theoretical orientation, which will make you accountable for the therapeutic work you do with clients.

As a beginning counselor, you may decide or feel pressured to skip self-understanding and theoretical development and jump straight to applying goals and techniques. You rightfully want to know what to do, and you may believe that you should learn immediately how to help. Unfortunately, in many training programs discussing counseling techniques comes too early. In these programs, helpers often learn *how* to act as a counselor before they learn *who* they are as a counselor. This approach is often driven by the belief that counselors' training rests primarily on helping counselors know *what to do.* The widely accepted belief that the counselor is the true *instrument of change* runs the risk of forgetting that counseling is ultimately a unique, yet specified relationship. At a fundamental level, almost anyone can learn techniques. For example, the *empty-chair technique* requires that you ask clients to talk to someone (the empty chair) as though people were present, although they are not. This technique is utilized to help individuals through various therapeutic challenges. Using this technique requires very simple instructions that a nonprofessional can understand. However, the ways in which you as a helper follow up on this intervention and how you respond to the client are based in your theory. Consequently, you must be theory based before you can be technique driven.

As the counselor, you are the one who ultimately provides interventions that help your clients achieve their goals. Each theory and school of thought provides you with techniques and therapeutic goals that are appropriate given *your* values and *your* clients' needs. If you have successfully adopted a theoretical approach, your effectiveness as a helper will then rely on your ability to recognize with your clients their needs and to execute techniques congruent with your theory (e.g., Hansen, Rossberg, & Cramer, 1994). At this point, researchers and clinicians who have come before you have already done the work and research, and you simply have to consult their teachings and writings. In this endeavor, you will quickly learn that the various schools, theories, and interventions strive to meet the needs and characteristics of a diverse society.

FURTHER MULTICULTURAL CONCERNS

Theoretical approaches to counseling are widely incorporating multicultural issues. Integrating this trend into your counseling approach first requires an understanding of the term culture. *Culture* is ultimately the rules, values, symbols, and ideologies of an identified group of people (Srebalus & Brown, 2001). This general definition of culture should help you to see that within an interactive society are separate and unique cultures. To understand the implications of culture, you must first understand your own culture and have a general understanding of other cultures with which you work. The diversities of age, gender, race, socioeconomic class, religion, and sexual orientation have a major impact both on how relationships develop and mature and on the counselor-client relationship. Typically, literature focuses on how counselors may most effectively work with clients who represent a population that is different from their own. Unfortunately, most of the literature assumes that the counselor is of the dominant culture. However, not uncommonly counselors themselves represent various cultures.

For example, many counseling textbooks offer practical suggestions for working with gay, lesbian, bisexual, and transgendered clients. This forum stresses that helpers must be in touch with their values and biases, and it is vital that they consider the social environment pertinent to their clients (Ivey, Ivey, & Simek-Morgan, 1997). Furthermore, issues specific to these populations, such as discrimination and coming out, are addressed. However, little practical support exists for the counselor who is from an underrepresented population. The question, How can a counselor work with a *lesbian client*? is not unique and is addressed in the professional literature. However the question, How can a *lesbian counselor* work with a client? is often ignored. In an emerging field, helpers continue to build on the research and literature addressing the multicultural needs of their clients. However, counselors often struggle in addressing their own multicultural needs.

Counselors also come from a variety of cultures and backgrounds. Their life philosophy and values, which are a dramatic component of their counseling approach, do influence how they interact with clients and direct what they believe is important for their clients. The Intentional Theory Selection (ITS) model utilized throughout this text offers great benefits to counselors across cultures of race, gender, sexual orientation, abilities, religions, and age. As we have outlined, the foundation of this model begins with the identification of one's life philosophy. However, life philosophy is so deeply rooted in one's specific culture that to imagine separation seems ludicrous.

How people view the world is influenced greatly by their cultural experience and basically defines much of who they are. Because of this influence, as counselors we must not only embrace the diversity of our client population, but we must embrace the diversity within our field.

RESISTANCE TO THEORIES: ECLECTIC, INTEGRATED, OR JUST DON'T KNOW

Many beginning helping professionals do not subscribe to one specific theory but rather identify themselves as being eclectic or integrative. Evidence supports trends in this area. For example, many theories textbooks now include chapters that focus on eclectic and integrative approaches such as Lazurus's multimodal theory, Prochaska and DiClemente's transtheoretical model along with many others. This trend is further evidenced by surveys of mental health practitioners who when asked about their theoretical orientation identify as eclectic.

While it is plausible and pragmatic for clinicians to choose interventions from various schools of thought, this choice requires intentionality and a thorough working knowledge of the utilized theories. Unfortunately, students in some cases endorse eclectic theories without having the required knowledge and intentionality of seasoned practitioners.

Although not always the case, portraying oneself as eclectic is an "easy out" when one is asked about personal theory. We have heard several students express that while interviewing for clinical positions, they present themselves as eclectic in an attempt to avoid presenting a theory not endorsed by the interviewer. These students believe that there is a "right" answer and part of their interviewing success depends on their ability to show themselves as congruent with the interviewer or open to the interviewer's personal theory. Additionally, as you likely are observing, your theory is ultimately based on your life philosophy—*your* values and beliefs—that in many ways are highly personal. To offer up a specific theory, a revelation of yourself, places you in a vulnerable position that portrays you and puts you in a place where criticism may occur. Especially as a beginning counselor, you may find it frightening to say specifically to which theory you ascribe. If you state, "I am a feminist therapist," you may be questioned about what that means, what your beliefs are, and what interventions a feminist helper utilizes in therapy. By identifying yourself as grounded in a specific theory, you are making a statement of what you believe and ultimately who you are. For example, if we say we are a psychoanalytic therapists, you have the opportunity to make some assumptions about us. Consequently, some students feel safer saying, "I am eclectic."

Additional students have shared that their portrayal as eclectic allowed them to utilize interventions that they believed would work. They shared that this allowed them to be "themselves" and meet individual clients where they are. The helping professions do typically promote individuality, so the students' argument has some merit. However, if helpers do not orientate themselves with a founded theory, they are not in a place where they can justify their work with clients. By not justifying their approach, they thereby circumvent truly intentional, ethical counseling.

An additional struggle with eclectic approaches revolves around the issue of student supervision. Typically, counselor educators and clinical supervisors attempt to provide helpers in training with feedback that is based in the trainee's specific approach. To train effective and ethical helpers, educators and supervisors must give students feedback on their clinical work. When students adopt an eclectic model, providing specific feedback is difficult. Not uncommonly students endorse this paradigm of eclecticism to avoid targeted feedback. Students may do this not to avoid learning or even grading, but rather because they fear being evaluated as a helping professional.

This resistance to adopting a theoretical orientation can surface in many forms. While the purpose of this book is to help counselors dedicate themselves to a theory, it is also an attempt to advocate for the helping professions and increase the professionalism of their identities. For example, because of the impact of health-care reform and managed care, as a profession, we are constantly required to provide more justification for counseling and psychotherapy. If as professionals, helpers are unable to portray themselves as being theory driven, they run the risk of being seen as incompetent and unreimbursable. Thus each counselor's openness to having strong theoretical foundations adds to the professionalism of the counseling field.

DOES IT REALLY WORK?

Let us offer you an example where we supervised a counselor in training through a practicum experience. In this class, the students saw clients, while we had the opportunity to observe them through a one-way mirror and make calls into the session to offer suggestions and reflections. The student we observed, Carolyn, showed a great level of understanding of theory, and she demonstrated skills beyond what is typical of her level of training. She consistently demonstrated the ability to develop quick rapport with her clients and was keenly attuned to the affective world of her clients.

She was working with a college student who was experiencing social anxiety and was potentially struggling with test anxiety. Carolyn was doing great work with her client and was really helping the client to see herself in a new way. In session Carolyn was helping the client to examine what thoughts and events tend to trigger times of greatest anxiety. She was sharing her observations of her client's social skills. Although the client was verbally expressing a fear of others, she was being quite open and honest with the counselor Carolyn. During the session, Carolyn also encouraged the client by saying that she "would be okay." A segment of the session follows.

Carolyn: So, during times where you notice you have values in common with others, you feel the greatest sense of social confidence.

Client: Well, I guess, but I still find I don't know how to talk with others. I struggle, as I don't feel I can be open with others. I am scared, frightened, and feel I have nothing to offer. I feel others will look at me and laugh and see how . . . well, how stupid I am. I am not quick, and well, because of this I don't talk. I try to keep the focus off of me.

Carolyn: So then you back down as you feel you have little to offer.

Client: Yes, I cannot be open with others. I have never been able to be honest with others about how I feel and stuff.

Carolyn: So you feel you really struggle opening up to others.

Client: Well, yes, all of the time.

Carolyn: What is hard for me to understand is how you believe you are never honest, yet you have been very honest with me today . . . you have shared your vulnerabilities without shutting down.

Client: Well . . . (smiling). Yeah, I guess. Maybe I am not always able to see when I am being open.

Carolyn: Sorta like, sometimes you are able to do it but don't see it.

Client: Yeah!

Carolyn: You know I think you will be okay.

Following the session we listened to Carolyn's reflections and gave her feedback. During this experience we were shocked at Carolyn's appraisal of the session. Carolyn shared that she belived her statement, "*You know I think you will be okay*" was the most beneficial words during the session. However, in fact this interaction was the least grounded in theory. Carolyn went on to say, she felt that her statement, "*What is hard for me to understand is how you believe you are never honest, yet you have been very honest with me today . . . You have shared your vulnerabilities without shutting down,*" was completely a value statement that would have been better to not share and did not have a place in counseling. We were shocked at her appraisal, not only because Carolyn's statement was grounded in the existential approach's value of being authentic, but also because the client later shared that it was the most meaningful interaction she encountered during her course of therapy.

When we shared this discrepancy with Carolyn, she said, "*But, I am not a humanist.*" After exploration with Carolyn, we learned that she had adopted her theoretical approach, not based on her philosophy or worldview, but on, as she put it, "*the theory my last supervisor liked.*"

During the following weeks, we asked Carolyn if she would take a step back from her theory. We asked her to first identify her values and philosophy of life. As she did, many themes emerged, and these focused greatly on her belief that people know what is best for them and that being genuine with others is essential to meaningful relationships. These perspectives are the cornerstones of many humanistic approaches, and these new insights helped Carolyn to begin to build a theory that would not only be effective with clients but would enable her to have a theoretical approach that truly fit for her. Through this process she was able to find a theory that was more congruent with her values and a way to be theory driven, while incorporating herself in the session. Carolyn's confidence and skill level with clients continued to increase. Clearly, in her work with clients, Carolyn's new confidence and self-understanding were increasing her effectiveness and ultimately helping her clients. Carolyn found that the humanistic approach was a natural and effective way for her to be effective with clients. She found that she could be grounded in a theory that was congruent with her beliefs and truly allowed her actions in therapy to be founded upon her values.

WHAT TO TAKE HOME

Each helper brings individual qualities to the therapeutic process. Your religion, ethnicity, gender, and sociological background attribute much not only to whom you are as a person but also to how you serve as a counselor. Additionally, as an individual, how you interpret or make meaning of your experiences inevitably changes you. Your adoption of core values and beliefs affects not only you, but also your clients. Your theoretical orientation can help you conceptualize and intervene with clients in a way that is effective for the client while congruent with who you are.

The process of adopting a theory that truly fits for your own belief system is difficult, but possible. It is an ongoing process because new experiences continuously influence your beliefs and values. At times, learning more about yourself may even require you to give up what were once cardinal components of your counseling approach. Being a theory-based clinician is an ethical and essential step in a helper's development. Through self-inquiry and study, you can begin a journey that can help you to become an effective counselor whose actions are based not only in theory but truly sprout from your own beliefs. Discovering your own values, life philosophy, and view of counseling and psychotherapy is an important step in your professional identity. However, you must also identify the views, values, and life philosophy of your clients.

REFLECTION QUESTIONS

1. The following questions are designed to assist you as you begin to articulate your life philosophy: (a) What do you value? (b) What do you find meaningful? (c) What influences in your life have been most profound in shaping your life philosophy?

2. Of the five schools of thought described in the chapter (psychodynamic, behavioral, humanistic, pragmatic, and contemporary), which do you feel most knowledgeable about? Which one(s) would you like to learn more about?

3. Bring to mind three clinical techniques you currently possess (i.e. empty chair, free association, charting, education, confrontation). Identify the theory to which each technique belongs.

4. In recent counseling and psychotherapy research there has been a trend toward integrative and eclectic techniques. What about these approaches do you personally find attractive? What about these approaches do you personally find unattractive?

5. In examining the Intentional Theory Selection (ITS) model, identify the areas in which you (a) feel confident and (b) need additional education, information and/or experience.

CHAPTER THREE

TOP TEN WAYS TO FIND YOUR THEORETICAL ORIENTATION

There is a difference between a philosophy and a bumper sticker.
—Charles M. Schulz

Selecting your theoretical orientation in a purposeful manner requires both knowledge of counseling theories and self-knowledge. As presented earlier, learning about yourself and your own life philosophy is the first step in integrating a theory of counseling, and the Intentional Theory Selection (ITS) model serves as a roadmap to finding your theoretical orientation. However, the next step is to be active in learning about yourself and how this information influences what theory might best fit for you.

In the style of *Late Night with David Letterman*, we will give you the top ten ways to find your theoretical orientation. We believe each strategy can lead you closer to your theoretical orientation and that each is important in the overall process of developing your theoretical orientation.

1. Find yourself

2. Articulate your values

3. Survey your preferences

4. Use your personality

5. Capture yourself

6. Let others inspire you in your learning

7. Read original works

8. Get real

9. Study with a master

10. Broaden your experiences

FIND YOURSELF

In order to choose a theoretical orientation that best fits you, you need to consider your own values, life philosophy, and worldview in an honest way. As helpers, all may aspire to provide unconditional positive regard and respect for clients, but the reality of clients' lives and behaviors may make that difficult to accomplish. Thus, we encourage you to be thoughtful and honest as you participate in the following activities designed to help you examine your values. You may find journaling about your values and reactions to the following questions helpful. Kottler (1999, p. 28) offers some important considerations that might help you become more familiar with your own values.

What do you see as the timeframe of counseling? Are you more oriented to the past, present, or future? To take this a step further, do you believe counseling is intended to work on current issues and feelings or to help people with issues and feelings from their past? Or, do you believe that people need to focus on their future feelings, thoughts, and behaviors?

What is your view of people? Do you believe people are essentially good, bad, or neutral? Do you believe clients are good people with issues to work out? Conversely, are your clients bad people with an inherent defect that requires counseling? Are people somewhere in between, such as good people that do bad things?

Who is in charge? Is the counselor in charge of the therapy or is the role shared equally with the client? If the role is shared, how much of it belongs to the client and how much belongs to the counselor? If the counselor is in charge, how is that established? How do you view your role as a counselor? Are you an expert, consultant, or friend?

What do you want the client to learn? Is the emphasis of counseling to gain insight, action, or both? Are you comfortable with clients leaving counseling with insight about their behaviors and feelings? Or, do you want the client to have insight and then "do" something with it? Do you pay attention to thoughts, feelings, behavior or all of them?

These questions will help you examine your values as they relate to the counseling process. As you think about the questions, write down your answers, which can help you identify your theoretical orientation. Your values as they relate to the helping process are just one way to examine yourself. To get a complete picture of your values as they relate to the helping process, you need to examine your counseling related values and your personal values. You will examine your personal values more in the next step.

ARTICULATE YOUR VALUES

We have developed some questions to assist you in examining your values and life philosophy. To begin the journey of introspection and imagination that will lead you to uncover your own value system and life philosophy, consider your honest answers to the following.

■ *The Funeral.* Imagine that you have been transported through time to your own funeral where your family and all the friends in your life have gathered. As part of the ceremony, an open microphone is provided for people who want to speak out their remembrances of you.

What do you think people would have to say about you? What would you like them to be able to say?

_____

_____

_____

■ *Free Week.* Imagine that suddenly you have been given one magical week of "free" life—you do not have to take care of tasks at work, finances, family, and household responsibilities. No backlog would accumulate. You would reenter the year at exactly the same time you left it, but you would have seven days for yourself. It would be as though the calendar just for you had fifty-three weeks.

What would you do? Who, if anyone, would you include?

_____

_____

_____

■ *Change.* Imagine that you have been given the power to *permanently* change three things about yourself.

What three things would you choose to change? Why?

_____

_____

_____

What would you change in your neighborhood? In your town? In your city? Why?

_____

_____

_____

What would you change if your power was extended to people in general? Why?

_____

_____

_____

If your power was now extended to the world, what would you choose to change permanently? Why?

_____

_____

_____

How do your views of multiculturalism and diversity relate to the things you selected to permanently change about the city? About the state? About the world in which you live?

_____

_____

_____

Review your answers to the personal values questions and then answer the following questions:

- What themes emerged from your answers?
- How are the changes that you strive for related to the changes that you hope your clients will make?
- What are your priorities?
- How are those priorities related to the way you work with clients?
- What kind of changes do you want to make for yourself and the world around you?
- How do these changes impact your role as a helping professional?

SURVEY YOUR PREFERENCES WITH THE SELECTIVE THEORY SORTER (STS)

Now that you have had a chance to reflect on your priorities and values as a person and a professional, you can participate in a survey that we developed to help you determine your theoretical orientation. The Selective Theory Sorter (STS) survey items are based on a literature review of numerous paramount counseling books and articles (e.g., Corey, 2004; Doyle, 1998; Ivey & Ivey, 1999; Jackson & Thompson, 1971; Young, 1998). The survey is designed to give you insight into your theoretical preferences and assess your views of pathology, the counseling process, and treatment modalities. It is not designed to be a diagnostic tool, but rather another tool for your self-exploration. (See pages 25–30.)

USE YOUR PERSONALITY

Your personality type can help guide you toward a theoretical orientation. The Myers-Briggs Type Indicator (MBTI) can be another way for you to understand your way of viewing the world (Myers & Myers, 1977). If you do not know your Myers-Briggs type, you might find it helpful to take the test, which is typically offered at career services offices on college campuses.

SELECTIVE THEORY SORTER [STS]

Read the following statements and indicate the strength of your beliefs in the white box following the statement. Your response for each item can range from -3 to $+3$ depending on the extent to which you believe a statement is not at all like you (-3) to a lot like you ($+3$). For example: If you believe the statement presented in item 30, "people are sexual beings," is a lot like your view of counseling, your answer might look like this:

	Not at all like me			Neutral			A lot like me		
	-3	-2	-1	0			1	2	3

30. People are sexual beings. → **3**

	Not at all like me			Neutral			A lot like me		
	-3	-2	-1	0			1	2	3

	A	B	C	D	E	F	G	H	I	J	K	L
1. A counselor should use bits and pieces from different theoretical systems of counseling and psychotherapy that can be integrated.											☐	
2. A major goal of therapy should be to assist the client in reaching a stage of unconditional self-acceptance by changing irrational beliefs.								☐				
3. A warm relationship between the therapist and client is not a necessary or sufficient condition for effective personality change.												
4. Behavior is a way to control perceptions.									☐			
5. Behavior is both consciously and unconsciously motivated by the environment and psychic energy.			☐									
6. Childhood events are the baseline for adult personality.	☐											
7. Childhood sexual attractions toward parents are responsible for later neurotic symptoms.	☐											
8. Clients are capable of imagining which behaviors are desirable and then working to make those images a behavioral reality.							☐					

	A	B	C	D	E	F	G	H	I	J	K	L
9. Clients must take ultimate responsibility for the way their life is lived.												X
10. Coming to grips with the unconscious part of the personality is the only way to truly achieve individuation.			X									
11. Dream interpretation, free association, hypnotic techniques, and fantasizing are good ways of gaining access to the client's unconscious.	X											
12. Each person determines the essence of his or her existence.					X							
13. Each person is unique and has the ability to reach full potential.				X								
14. Everyone is unique.				X								
15. Feelings are neither good nor bad but are events, facts of our existence, real, and indisputable.						X						
16. Feelings may be changed through knowledge of their origin followed by a change in behavior.						X						
17. Goals of therapy should include assisting the client in learning the consciousness of their responsibility, to bring unconscious spiritual factors to the conscious, and to recover meaning to existence.												X
18. How a person thinks largely determines how one feels and behaves.										X		
19. Human problems stem *not* from external events or situations but from people's view or beliefs about them.							X					
20. Humans are constantly striving to maintain equilibrium.					X							
21. Humans are pulled by the future and are self-controlled.		X										
22. Humans strive for actualization—to maintain or promote growth.				X								
23. Irrational beliefs are the principal of emotional disturbance.									X			
24. It is important to fulfill one's needs, and to do so in a way that does not deprive others of the ability to fulfill their needs.									X			

	A	B	C	D	E	F	G	H	I	J	K	L
25. Maladaptive behaviors, like adaptive behaviors, are learned. They can also be unlearned.												
26. Maladjusted behavior results in losing effective control over perceptions and over entire lives.									☐			
27. Maladjustment can be determined by the degree of disturbance between personality constructs.						☐						
28. Movement toward psychological growth and self-actualizing is often sabotaged by self-defeating thoughts.								☐				
29. Mutual trust, acceptance, and spontaneity are important when building the counselor/client relationship.				☐								
30. People are sexual beings.	☐											
31. People control what they believe, not what actually exists.								☐				
32. People have both internal and external definitions of themselves.										☐		
33. People have the need to survive and reproduce—basic biological needs.					☐							
34. Personality development is founded more on a progression of learned cognitions than on biological predispositions.										☐		
35. Personality is acquired through the use of negative and/or positive reinforcers.							☐					
36. Personality is constructed through the attribution of meaning.												☐
37. Providing genuineness, unconditional positive regard, and empathic understanding are essential to promote growth in the client.				☐								
38. Recognizing cognitive processing in emotion and behavior is central in therapy.								☐				
39. Social urges take precedence over sexual urges in personality development.		☐										
40. Successful adaptation to life depends on the degree of social interest in goal striving.		☐										
41. The central focus of counseling should be the client's experiencing of feelings.				☐								

	A	B	C	D	E	F	G	H	I	J	K	L
42. The conscious rather than unconscious is the primary source of ideas and values.		☐										
43. The counselor should assume that the client is the expert on his or her problems.											☐	
44. The human personality consists of three "figures": child, parent, and adult.						☐						
45. The integration of the total person in his or her own unique field is essential in therapy.					☐							
46. The major goal of therapy is the gaining of client autonomy.						☐						
47. The past determines the present, even though human motivation should be focused on the future.			☐									
48. The process of individuation and self-realization should be the goal of living and of therapy.			☐									
49. The purpose of therapy is to bring the unconscious to the conscious.	☐											
50. The role in the family is one of the biggest influences in determining the personality characteristics of the client.		☐										
51. The unconscious contains more than repressed material; it is a place of creativity, guidance, and meaning.			☐									
52. The ways people form, organize, and interpret their basic cognitive structures determine how they will perceive and behave.										☐		
53. Therapy is unique, humanistic, cognitive, and existential.											☐	
54. Therapy should be here-and-now based, where every moment of life matters.											☐	
55. Therapy should focus on living more honestly and being less caught up in trivialities.											☐	
56. There are no underlying causes for maladjustment. Maladjustive behavior can be directly defined and attacked.							☐					

	A	B	C	D	E	F	G	H	I	J	K	L
57. There is no one best approach or strategy when it comes to therapy.												
58. There is no one true path to effective psychotherapy.												
59. There is no such thing as free will or voluntary behavior.												
60. Viewing an event or situation out of context is one of the systematic errors in cognitive reasoning.												
Column Totals												

SCORING THE SELECTIVE THEORY SORTER [STS]

Use the following instructions to score the STS:

1. To score the STS, add the scores in each column on each page. Be sure to accurately count both positive and negative numbers.
2. Transfer the column totals to the corresponding theories listed below.

THEORY	**TOTAL SCORE**
A. Psychoanalytic	_____
B. Adlerian	_____
C. Jungian	_____
D. Client-centered	_____
E. Gestalt	_____
F. Transactional analysis	_____
G. Behaviorism	_____
H. REBT	_____
I. Reality	_____
J. Cognitive-behavioral	_____
K. Integrative	_____
L. Existential	_____

3. To determine the specific theory or theories that are most appealing to you, find the two or three of your highest column scores and list them here:

THEORY	**TOTAL SCORE**
_____	_____
_____	_____
_____	_____

EXPLANATION OF SCORING

The Selective Theory Sorter is based on a comprehensive review of literature surrounding counseling theories. The items contained in the STS reflect the beliefs inherent in each school of thought. Currently, no published psychometric properties are attached to the STS. Rather, it is a survey that is intended for self-discovery.

The two or three theories you found most appealing and scored the highest are those that likely match with your life philosophy as it is today. These theories are, however, only preferences. For example, if you had two theories that tied, then you might need to examine and read about them in more depth. Additionally, you may have discovered that your preferences match a theory with which you are unfamiliar. Regardless of your results, you might find that looking in greater depth at the theories you identified gives you a better understand of the theories and confidence in your ability to select one.

The Myers-Briggs Type Indicator is a commonly used measure that examines personality characteristics. Developed by Isabel Briggs Myers and Katherine Briggs in the 1950s, the MBTI is theoretically conceptualized from a personal wellness perspective versus a pathology comparison model. All scores obtained on the MBTI are seen as appropriate and acceptable ways of interacting with the environment and emphasize the traits or characteristics that support the balance of the individual's psychological personality system. The MBTI is a forced-choice, self-report inventory that classifies individuals into one of sixteen personality types, each with a unique set of characteristics and tendencies (Willis, 1989). According to Myers and McCaulley (1985), the main objective of the MBTI is to identify a combination of four basic preferences that determine type. An individual receives a four-letter code type determined by their scores on four theoretically independent dimensions. Each dimension has two dichotomous preferences with only one preference from each categorization ascribed to any one individual (Willis, 1989).

The first dimension is the Introversion/Extroversion (E/I) index. The E/I index is designed to reflect whether a person is an extravert or an introvert. An *extravert* is defined as a person who directs energy and attention to the outer world and receives energy from external events, experiences, and interactions (Myers, 1998). An *introvert* prefers to focus on the inner world of ideas and impressions, thoughts, feelings, and reflections (Myers, 1998).

Sensing/iNtuition (S/N) is the second index. The S/N index reflects a person's preference between two opposite ways of perceiving, sensing, or intuiting. A person who relies primarily upon the process of sensing (S), reports observable facts or happenings through one or more of the five senses. According to Myers (1998), people with sensing preferences observe the world around them and are skilled at recognizing the practical realities of a situation. A person who responds more to iNtuition (N), reports meanings, relationships, and/or possibilities that have been worked out beyond the reach of the conscious mind. Those who prefer intuition see the big picture, focusing on connections, understandings, and relationships between facts (Myers, 1998).

The third dimension is the Thinking/Feeling (T/F) index. The T/F index describes a person's preference between two contrasting ways of judgment. A person who typically reacts from a thinking (T) perspective to make decisions on the basis of logical consequences, or objective truth is identified as a Thinking (T) type. Thinking relies on principles of cause and effect and tends to be impersonal (Myers & McCaulley,

1985). People associated with Thinking (T) may develop characteristics associated with analytical ability, objectivity, and concern with justice and fairness.

In contrast, a person who operates based on Feeling (F) makes decisions on the basis of personal or social values with the goal of harmony and recognition of the individual (Myers, 1993). Feeling-type people support their decisions with an understanding of personal values and group values, and thus they tend to be more subjective than thinking-type people. Feeling-types tend to be people oriented and are characterized as having concern with the human, a need for affiliation, a capacity for warmth, and a desire for harmony (Myers & McCaulley, 1985).

The fourth dimension is the Judging/Perceiving (J/P) index. The J/P index describes the process a person uses in dealing with the outer world—the extraverted part of life. A person who prefers judgment (J) uses one of the judgment processes of thinking or feeling for dealing with the outside world. Perceiving (P) types tend to operate from a sensing or intuition perspective when dealing with the outside world.

Because counselors tend to select counseling theories that fit their own personality styles, you may find research regarding the MBTI and theoretical orientation helpful in your quest for a theoretical orientation (Erickson, 1993). The Thinking/Feeling preference on the MBTI is particularly illuminating when examining theoretical orientation. Thinking types tend to interact with others in a task-oriented, analytic, and objective manner. Feeling types tend to focus on personal values, subjective viewpoints, and people-oriented discussions. Thus, thinking types are disproportionately likely to choose predominantly cognitive theories such as Adlerian, behavioral, REBT, and reality therapy. Feeling types are more likely to choose predominantly affective approaches such as Gestalt, existential, and client-centered.

Though the MBTI is recommended in this text, many other personality inventories may be helpful to you in your mission toward self-discovery. We chose the MBTI because it has been researched as it relates to theory selection among counselors and psychotherapists.

CAPTURE YOURSELF

Audio and videotaping techniques are valuable ways to capture yourself working as a professional helper. Taping techniques can show you whether or not your counseling skills actually convey your theory. Ideally, the theoretical orientation you espouse will be one that is easily recognizable on tape so that you can determine whether your interventions, strategies, and ways of relating to your client are congruent with your theoretical orientation. Sometimes, viewing a tape is the first time students in the helping professions recognize that their intended theoretical orientation is not apparent in the counseling session. Thus, taping can help you track your progress toward intentional counseling and use of theory in the helping relationship. Additionally, taping yourself provides an opportunity for you to receive feedback from others who can assist you in understanding whether or not your clinical work is reflective of the theoretical orientation you espouse.

LET OTHERS INSPIRE YOU IN YOUR LEARNING

In a number of ways others can inspire you in your learning. This book, which gives you an opportunity to examine your theoretical orientation, is a launching pad for exploring your role as a professional helper. Professional conferences and other professional development opportunities, which you can attend, may also help. The most well-regarded people in the field often conduct workshops that can help you better understand theory and therapeutic techniques. To get involved in these educational opportunities, ask your faculty members, supervisors, and colleagues about the professional organizations to which they belong. You can find numerous professional growth opportunities at the state, regional, national, and international levels.

READ ORIGINAL WORKS

Theories textbooks offer a wealth of information about various theories. However, each time a theory is paraphrased, something is lost. Thus, we recommend that you read as many works by the original theorists as possible. The recommended reading list on page 35 is organized around the five schools of thought presented in Chapter 4. The list is not all encompassing but is intended to get you started.

GET REAL

Another way you can solidify your theoretical orientation is to put it to the test with some real-world trials. As you conduct the activities of your everyday life, try out your theoretical orientation with people in all sorts of situations and backgrounds. For example, one professional counselor had what she called a "typical Saturday." She spent her day going to the grocery store, getting a haircut, and attending a cultural event. The counselor reported that while getting her hair cut, she interacted with a 20-year-old, Caucasian hairdresser who was expecting her second child and was unsure of her relationship with the child's father. At the grocery store, the counselor interacted with a cashier in a wheelchair, and later she met a Bosnian house painter who was a highly regarded artist in Bosnia before the war. In each of these situations, the counselor had the opportunity to monitor whether or not her humanistic leanings worked in her every day life. The counselor noticed that she was able to have unconditional, positive regard for each of the people with whom she interacted. She also noted that she was not able to be genuine with each person she encountered but decided that her response was okay since each of these relationships were not personal or counseling in nature. The counselor's experience illustrates the importance of finding a theoretical orientation that fits your personality. Because the theoretical orientation you espouse will ideally resonate with your being in most situations, you need one that fits with who you are both inside and outside of the therapeutic relationship.

STUDY WITH A MASTER

One of the best ways to learn a theoretical approach to the helping professions is to study with a master or at an institute specializing in the theory in which you are interested. These opportunities will allow you to study with the creator of the theory or with some of the creator's protégés. Regardless of how you obtain additional education about a specific theory that education will help you establish a theoretical orientation that fits for you. You can find many training opportunities both inside and outside of the United States. Although you would need an immense amount of time to study at all institutes, you can pick experiences that are most appealing to you by reading original works and learning more about yourself, you can. The following Websites contain information that can get you started.

Aaron T. Beck Center for Cognitive Therapy, 3600 Market St , Philadelphia, PA 19101, (215) 898-4100: www.uphs.upenn.edu/psycct/images/cctmain.jpg

Albert Ellis Institute: www.rebt.org

Association for Humanistic Psychology: www.ahpweb.org

Association for the Advancement of Gestalt Therapy: www.aagt.org

Center for the Studies of the Person (based on Carl Roger's work): www.centerfortheperson.org

Feminist Therapy Institute: www.feministtherapyinstitute.org

Feminist Therapy: Jean Baker Miller Institute at the Stone Center of Wellesley College: www.wellesley.edu/JBMTI

International Network on Personal Meaning: www.meaning.ca

International Transactional Analysis Association: www.itaap-net.org

Multicultural Counseling and Consulting Center: www.4mccc.com

Narrative Therapy: www.narrativeapproaches.com

National Multicultural Institute: www.nmci.org

Solution Focused: www.possibilities.com

The Rollo May Center for Humanistic Studies: www.saybrook.edu

Viktor Frankl Institute of Vienna: www.logotherapy.univie.ac.at

William Glasser Institute: www.wglasserinst.com

BROADEN YOUR EXPERIENCES

The best way to expose yourself to new ideas and situations is by living outside of your comfort zone, which may entail learning about cultures different from your own. Experiences outside of your comfort zone not only allow you to encounter diverse thoughts, they also allow you to compare your own beliefs to those unique to others. This may help you in articulating your worldview and anchoring your beliefs in cultures around you. To accomplish this, you may need to work with and experience a variety of clients' issues, which you can do in several ways. First, try to get experience working in a wide variety of settings. Spend time working with people of ethnicities, cultural backgrounds, and socioeconomic status that are different from your own. For example, if you are a mental-health or community counselor, spend time working with adults, kids, and families to expose yourself to as many diverse experiences as possible. If you are a school counselor, you may choose to get experience working with elementary, middle-school, and high-school students. Ideally, you would glean this experience in schools that are different from one another.

Second, you may want to study abroad. Valuable opportunities in learning about counseling and about other cultures are available through many graduate programs that offer multicultural and theories courses in other countries. You might seek grant funding such as a Fulbright scholarship to study the helping professions in another country. You can also have multicultural experiences without ever leaving the country. Many universities have organized, international student groups where you can volunteer to be a conversation partner or to host an international student. These opportunities can add diversity to your day-to-day life.

TOP TEN WRAP UP

The helping professions are unique from many other fields because self-understanding is essential to a job well done. To be an effective therapist, you must have a working theory to guide how you serve clients. Self-insight is the first step in the process of finding a theoretical orientation, and the key to finding your theoretical orientation is understanding your life philosophy. A few of the ways to gain greater self-understanding include finding your values, understanding your preferences, and having new experiences.

Engaging in activities that help you with personal insight can make you a better professional, which consequently, contributes to your effectiveness in your work with clients. Your intentionality ultimately will help you find a theory that is congruent with your values not only as a professional but also as a person. Obviously, this will likely lead to a career you find more fulfilling.

In Chapter 4, we present some theories and explain how they fit with the ITS model. Then, in Chapter 5, we provide some examples of students who utilized the ITS model to aid them in their professional development. These individuals, diverse like the clients they now serve, went through similar, universal struggles that are common with those beginning in the helping field. We hope their experiences will help you in your own process.

REFLECTION QUESTIONS

1. In this chapter you were asked to complete some exercises to articulate your values. What did you learn about yourself? How will you integrate your learning into your quest for a theoretical orientation?

2. After reviewing your results on the Selective Theory Sorter (STS), which theories did you find most appealing? Least appealing? What are your thoughts on your results?

3. How do your current theories of choice match up with your personality or MBTI type?

4. Evaluate one of your counseling sessions on video or audio tape. How do your skills demonstrate your current theoretical orientation? In what areas do you need improvement? Who can you ask to assist you in making sure your skills match your stated theoretical orientation?

5. In your search to ascertain a theoretical orientation, which original works do you plan to read? Which opportunities to study with a master are most appealing to you? How will you obtain these experiences? When?

SUGGESTED READINGS

PSYCHODYNAMIC

Adler, A. (1998). *What life could mean to you.* Center City, MN: Hazelden Information Education.
Adler, A., Ansbacher, H. L, & Ansbacher, R. R. (1989). *Individual psychology of Alfred Adler: A systematic presentation in selections from his writings.* New York: HarperCollins.
Freud, S. (1966, original work published 1920). *A general introduction to psychoanalysis.* New York: W.W. Norton.
Freud, S., & Strachey, J. (editor). (1983). *Interpretation of dreams.* Asheville, NC: Avon.
Freud, S., Strachey, J., & Gay, P. (1975). *Group psychology and the analysis of the ego.* New York: W.W. Norton.
Freud, S., Strachey, J., & Gay, P. (1990). *Beyond the pleasure principle.* New York: W.W. Norton.
Horney, K. (1991). *Neurosis and human growth: The struggle toward self-realization.* New York: W.W. Norton.
Horney, K. (1994). *The neurotic personality of our time.* New York: W.W. Norton.
Jung, C. (1958). *Psychology and religion.* New York: Pantheon.
Jung, C. (1965). *Memories, dreams, reflections.* New York: Vintage Books.

BEHAVIORISM

Skinner, B. F. (1976). *About behaviorism.* New York: Random House.
Skinner, B. F. (1976). *Walden two.* Boston: Allyn & Bacon.
Skinner, B. F. (2002). *Beyond freedom & dignity.* Indianapolis, IN Hackett Publishing Company.

HUMANISTIC APPROACHES

Frankl, V. (1967). *Psychotherapy and existentialism: Selected papers on Logotherapy.* New York: Washington Square Press.
Frankl, V. (1969) *The will to meaning.* New York: New American Library.
Frankl, V. (1985). Logos, paradox, and the search for meaning. In M. J. Mahoney & A. Freeman (Eds.). *Cognition and psychotherapy* (pp. 259–275). New York: Plenum.
Frankl, V. (1985). *The unheard cry for meaning: Psychotherapy and humanism.* New York: Simon & Shuster.
Frankl, V. (1992). *Man's search for meaning: An introduction to Logotherapy* (3rd ed). New York: Oxford University Press.
Maslow, A. (1962). *Toward a psychology of being.* New York: Van Nostrand.
Maslow, A. (1971). *The farther reaches of human nature.* New York: Viking.
May, R. (1958). The origins and significance of the existential movement in psychology. In R. May, E. Angel, & H. Ellenberger (Eds.), *Existence* (pp. 3–36). New York: Basic Books.
May, R. (Ed.). (1961). *Existential psychology.* New York: Random House.
May, R. (1969). *Love and will.* New York: W.W. Norton.
May, R. (1983) *The discovery of being: Writings in existential psychology.* New York: W.W. Norton.

May, R. (1992 [1939]). *The art of counseling.* London: Souvenir Press.

Perls, F. (1969). *Gestalt therapy verbatim.* Moab, UT: Real People's Press.

Perls, F. (1969). *In and out of the garbage pail.* Moab, UT: Real People's Press.

Perls, F. (1973). *The Gestalt approach and eye witness to therapy.* Palo Alto, CA: Science & Behavior Books.

Rogers, C. (1951) *Client-centered therapy: Its current practice, implications, and theory.* Boston: Houghton Mifflin.

Rogers, C. (1957). The necessary and sufficient conditions of therapeutic personality change. *Journal of Consulting Psychology, 21,* 95–103.

Rogers, C. (1961). *On becoming a person.* Boston: Houghton-Mifflin.

Rogers, C. (1969). *Freedom to learn.* Columbus, OH: Merrill.

Rogers, C. (1970). *On encounter groups.* New York: HarperCollins.

Rogers, C. (1972). *Becoming partners.* New York: Delta.

Rogers, C. (1977). *On personal power.* New York: Delacourt.

Rogers, C. (1980). *A way of being.* Boston: Houghton-Mifflin.

Rogers, C. (1995). *On becoming a person: A therapist's view of psychotherapy.* Boston: Houghton Mifflin.

Rogers, C., & Wallen, J. (1946). *Counseling with returned servicemen.* New York: McGraw-Hill.

Yalom, I. (1980). *Existential psychotherapy.* New York: Basic Books.

Yalom, I. (1990). *Love's Executioner and other tales of psychotherapy.* New York: Basic Books.

Yalom, I. (2001). *The Gift of therapy.* New York: HarperCollins.

PRAGMATIC APPROACHES

Beck, A. T. (1976). *Cognitive therapy and the emotional disorders.* New York: International Universities Press.

Beck, A. (1991). Cognitive therapy: A 30-year retrospective. *American Psychologist, 46,* 368–375.

Beck, J. S., & Beck, A. T. (1995). *Cognitive therapy: Basics and beyond.* New York: Guilford.

Burns, D. D. (1999). *The feeling good handbook.* New York: Plume.

Burns, D. D. (1999). *Feeling good: The new mood therapy.* New York: Wholecare.

Ellis, A. (1958). *Sex without guilt.* Secaucus, NJ: Lyle Stuart.

Ellis, A. (1971). *Growth through reason.* Palo Alto, CA: Science and Behavior Books.

Ellis, A. (1983). The origins of rational-emotive therapy (RET). *Voices, 18,* 29–33.

Ellis, A. (1994). *Reason and emotion in psychotherapy.* New York: Birch Lane.

Ellis, A. (1995). Changing rational-emotive therapy to rational-emotive behavior therapy. *Journal of Rational-Emotive and Cognitive-Behavior Therapy, 13,* 85–90.

Ellis, A. (1996). *Reason and emotion in psychotherapy.* New York: Carol Publishing Group.

Ellis, A. (1998). *How to make yourself happy and remarkably less disturbable.* San Luis Obispo, CA: Impact.

Ellis, A. (1999). Rational-emotive behavior therapy as an internal control psychology. *International Journal of Reality Therapy, 19,* 4–11.

Ellis, A. (2000). A continuation of the dialogue on issues in counseling in the postmodern era. *Journal of Mental Health Counseling, 22,* 97–106.

Glasser, W. (1965). *Reality therapy.* New York: HarperCollins.

Glasser, W. (1998). *Choice theory: A new psychology of personal freedom.* New York: HarperPerennial.

Kelly, G. (1955). *The psychology of personal constructs* (Vols. 1 and 2). New York: W.W. Norton.

Meichenbaum, D. (1977). *Cognitive-behavior modification: An integrative approach.* New York: Plenum Press.

Meichenbaum, D. (1985). *Stress inoculation training.* Boston: Allyn & Bacon.

CONTEMPORARY APPROACHES

Multicultural Counseling and Therapy

Atkinson, D., Morten, G., & Sue, D. W. (1997). *Counseling American minorities.* New York: McGraw-Hill.

Pontorotto, J., Casas, J. M., Suzuki, L. A., & Alexander, C. (2001). *Handbook of multicultural counseling.* Thousand Oaks, CA: Sage Publications.

Sue, D. W. (2003). *Overcoming our racism: The journey to liberation.* New York: John Wiley & Sons.

Sue, D. W. & Sue, D. (2003). *Counseling the culturally diverse: Theory and practice.* New York: John Wiley & Sons.

Feminist Approaches

Enns, C. Z. (1993). Twenty years of feminist counseling and therapy: From naming biases to implementing multi-faceted practice. *The Counseling Psychologist, 21* (1), 3–87.

Gilligan, C. (1993). *In a different voice: Psychological theory and women's development.* Cambridge, MA: Harvard University Press.

Miller J. B. (Ed.), (1973). *Psychoanalysis and women.* Baltimore, Penguin Books.

Miller, J. B. (1976). *Toward a new psychology of women.* Boston: Beacon Press.

Miller, J. B., & Stiver, I. P. (1997). *The healing connection: How women form relationships in therapy and in life.* Boston: Beacon Press.

Miller, J. B., & Welch A. S. (1995). Learning from women. In P. Chesler, E. D. Rothblum, & E. Cole (Eds.), *Feminist foremothers in women's studies, psychology, and mental health* (pp. 335–346). New York: The Haworth Press.

Solution Focused

Berg, K. B. (2003). *Children's solution work.* New York: W. W. Norton & Company.

De Shazer, S. (1985). *Keys to solution in brief therapy.* New York: W. W. Norton & Company.

CHAPTER FOUR

FIVE SCHOOLS OF THOUGHT AND THEIR THEORIES OF HELPING

If we value the pursuit of knowledge, we must be free to follow wherever that search may lead us. The free mind is not a barking dog, to be tethered on a ten-foot chain.

—Adlai E. Stevenson, 1952

We hope you that now have an understanding of how the Intentional Theory Selection model can help you incorporate your theoretical orientation into practice. Additionally, you may have begun to see how your own values affect your choice of a theoretical orientation and to consider how these values may influence your role as a helping professional. We now present five schools of related thought along with specific theories that often serve as the icons for each school. Each theory is presented following the ITS model.

First, each school will be outlined with a general overview. Following, each specific theory is a review of the theory's philosophy, goals, and techniques that will serve as a reminder of the key components of each theory and the actions it suggests for working with clients. Consequently, each theory will be examined with respect to how it fits with the ITS model. Additionally, one example of a person's ITS is shown within each school of thought. This will allow you to see how a sampling of counselors and psychotherapists would view the development of their own theoretical orientations.

This chapter is meant to serve as either a reminder of the main components of various theories to which you have been exposed or as a primer enticing you to look further at theories you may not completely understand. As we presented in Chapter 3, you can gain a greater appreciation and understanding for specific theories in many ways. Processes such as reading original works, surveying your preferences through such tools as the Selective Theory Sorter (STS), or studying with a master can provide you with the depth of understanding you need or want to truly integrate your own theoretical orientation and to help individual clients in a therapeutic setting. Most theories presented also have specific goals and techniques applicable to working in therapeutic group and family-therapy settings. Group and family therapy are typically

TABLE 4.1 ITS-Style Summary of Theories

THEORY	PHILOSOPHY OF PEOPLE	SCHOOL	MAJOR THEORISTS	GOALS	COMMON TECHNIQUES
Psychoanalytic	Humans are sexual, hedonistic and pleasure seeking; the unconcious is key to behavior; deconstructive; deterministic; developmental	Psychodynamic	Sigmund Freud; Anna Freud; Karen Horney	Insight; understanding; moving through past hurts; uncover the unconscious	Free association; dream analysis; interpretation; analysis of transference
Analytical Psychology	Humans connected ancestrally; holistic; spiritual; life-long development; biological drives important	Psychodynamic	Carl Jung	Individuation of the self; analysis of the psyche; archetypal understanding; personality integration	Insight; education; warm relationship; catharsis; dream analysis; archetypal analysis
Individual Psychology	Humans are social beings; holistic view of people; all behavior is goal directed; people have free will and are creative	Psychodynamic	Alfred Adler	Increase social interest; understand personal private logic and goals	Therapeutic alliance; learning client's lifestyle; collect early recollections
Transactional Analysis	People interact from three distinct development (ego) states; people seek attention; childhood survival influences current behavior	Psychodynamic	Eric Berne; Thomas Harris	Increase personal balance; understanding of ego states; change life scripts	Analysis; psychoeducation; contractual; egalitarian relationship; understanding
Behavioral	Empirical; behavior is an environmental product; present focused; scientific; people are hedonistic	Behavioral	B. F. Skinner	Environmental change; specific behavioral change	Education; reinforcement scheduling; modeling; systematic desensitization; relaxation techniques; assertiveness and skills training; charting; aversion therapy
Client Centered	Humans strive to self-actualize; phenomenological; present is important	Humanistic	Carl Rogers	Self-actualization; increase congruence	Genuineness; unconditional positive regard; empathy
Existential	Finding life meaning is important; anxiety based in core life conditions; people are free; phenomenological	Humanistic	Viktor Frankl; Irvin Yalom	Awareness; self-actualization; gaining responsibility; acceptance of core conditions of life; create/find meaning in life	Relationship based; empathy; client understanding; meaning identification

Theory	Key Concepts	Category	Key Figures	Goals	Techniques
Gestalt	Holistic; future focused; experiential	Humanistic	Fritz Perls	Integration; gain self-responsibility	Awareness; empty chair; use of pronouns; sharing hunches; dream work
Cognitive Therapy	Thinking and feeling are connected; people are creative	Pragmatic	Aaron Beck; David Burns	Change thinking; identify beliefs; awareness of automatic thoughts	Psychoeducation, collaborative relationship; behavioral techniques; cognitive modification
REBT	Humans have innate tendency towards actualization; tendency to focus on irrational thoughts	Pragmatic	Albert Ellis	Change thinking; reduce irrational thoughts; change value system	Education; confrontation; disputing irrational beliefs; homework; skill training
Reality Therapy	Humans strive to have needs met; all need survival, belonging, power, freedom, and fun	Pragmatic	William Glasser	Make effective choices; accept responsibility; understanding	Supportive relationship; contracts; create plans; pinning down; positive addicting behaviors
Multicultural Counseling	Culture based; belief systems important; problems may be external and cultural based	Contemporary	Derald Wing Sue; David Sue; Paul Pedersen; Patricia Arrerdondo	Cultural understanding; awareness of values and biases; understanding; change oppressive systems	Worldview consideration; self-aware; techniques vary consider client population
Feminist Theory	Oppressive systems contribute to women's psychosocial struggles; view women as positive	Contemporary	J. B. Miller; Carol Gilligan	Help client see the world in various ways; deconstruct traditional patriarchal culture	Egalitarian relationship; resource utilization; information sharing; personal validation challenge stereotypes
Narrative Therapy	People define themselves through stories; people are social; social constructivists; people have good intentions	Contemporary	Michael White	Change thinking and living; define self through positive stories	Collaborative relationship; finding exceptions; author new stories; increase choices; externalization story telling; metaphors
Solution Focused Brief Therapy	Change may occur in a short time; future based; phenomenological;	Contemporary	Insoo Kim Berg; Steve de Shazer	Identify problems and change them; identify ways problems are maintained	Miracle questions; finding exceptions; strength assessment

presented separately, which allows counselors and psychotherapists to first develop an orientation relevant to working with individual clients. This chapter will also emphasize the individual focus of each theory.

The authors of this book have identified over 250 theories of counseling and psychotherapy. Each theory has its unique strengths and limitations, and many theories stand alone as useful paradigms for client conceptualization and as a guide for offering therapeutic interventions. However, individual approaches often have much in common with other theories and may look very similar. Consequently, each theory fits into a family, or a *school of thought*. Each school of thought has related beliefs, with each individual member looking more or less like each other. The five schools presented in this chapter are: psychodynamic, behavioral, humanistic, pragmatic, and contemporary approaches. See Table 4.1 (p. 40) for a summary of each theory following the ITS model.

PSYCHODYNAMIC SCHOOL OF THOUGHT

The first and most historical school of thought is psychodynamic. In general, the psychodynamic school of thought—believes that human beings are basically driven by psychic energy and molded by early experiences. Unconscious motives and conflicts are central in current presenting behavior. These psychic forces are strong and individuals are thought to be driven by basic inherent impulses. Traditional psychoanalytic theory (primarily Sigmund Freud) views these impulses as solely sexual and aggressive. However, later theorists find strong motivations in other areas, such as socialization and individuation (a process of becoming whole). Development is of critical importance in psychodynamic approaches as later personality problems are often rooted in childhood experiences.

The view of therapy in both the traditional and later approaches is typically based on a complex understanding of the personality, or the *psyche*. Each of these approaches looks deeply at what defines human experience and, with a few expectations, what are the structures of the personality.

Therapeutic techniques are highly experiential and are typically considered to promote long-term, life-long change. Change is deep in nature and focused on insight and understanding. The therapeutic relationship is important. However, the insights offered are the primary precursors to change. The four icons of the psychodynamic approach are *psychoanalytic, analytical psychology, individual psychology* and *transactional analysis*.

Psychoanalytic Theory

Sigmund Freud is often considered the founding father of psychotherapy. Freud lived in a time where medical intervention was the basis of psychological treatment. However, he increased the availability and recognition of "talk therapy." Even in the layperson's world, Freud is known for identifying everything from slips of his own tongue to defense mechanisms. To paint even a small picture of Freud would take a lot of canvas to express his many layers and complexities. So, just the highlights are offered.

Philosophy.   Freud viewed the human world as filled with sexual impulses and deterministic ebbs. Freud basically believed that people struggle to balance complete animalistic and innate pleasure-seeking impulses with the challenges of social constraints (Gilliland & James, 1998). In addition, Freud believed that people must balance their repressed sexual and aggressive urges in order to feel and function in a healthy way.

Unfortunately, most of what people do is powered by *libidinal energy* that is hidden, deep in their unconscious. Libidinal energy is dynamic, in that it moves from various areas of conscious and unconscious, and it is limited. This energy, which is primarily sexual and aggressive, powers people's actions. However, most motivations and desires are beneath one's conscious awareness. Consequently, more often than not, when people experience psychological pain, they may not even know why. Freud believed that it was nearly impossible to directly "see" what is unconscious.

Freud was a deconstructivist; he broke minds down into "parts" that played different roles in psychological functioning. At the most basic, primal level, he identified the *id*. The id, powered by the *pleasure principle*, is one's biological baby who wants to be fed and have all needs, including eating, sleeping and especially sex, met at all times. The *ego*, however, works on the *reality principle*, attempting to deal with a social world with limited resources. The ego also serves as the mediator between the id and the moralistic *superego*. The superego strives to be perfect and is a person's personal, moralistic component. These components of a person's mind drive every behavior. However, each component has a developmental beginning. For example, the superego does not emerge at birth but develops as a person receives messages of right and wrong, typically from parents. Children's egos develop as they learn that they live in a world of limited resources (e.g., food only arrives when adults deliver it). And, one's id, which is present at birth, is innate and wants its needs met from day one.

As mentioned, psychoanalysis has a determinist view of life: Nothing happens without a reason, and the past causes our behaviors. Consequently, human personality is determined by early childhood experience. Freud identified specific *psychosexual stages* that all people experience. As people develop, what happens around them ultimately happens to them. People mature and move through development stages and are met with challenges along the way. If they successfully move through and meet these challenges, they typically will maintain a relative level of health. However, if their struggles are too great, they may always be slightly stuck at one stage, or, at the extreme, become fixated at early psychosocial stages. At each stage, people focus on hedonistic gratification. This primarily sexual gratification is a developmental stage: getting one's needs met (gratification) and the process by which this occurs. At each step of the way, people run the risk of being psychologically traumatized. To avoid psychological fear and pain, people often take experiences, fluid in their conscious mind, and push them deep down in their unconscious mind. However, these experiences remain in the mind, hidden by *defense mechanisms*. Defenses, such as projection and repression, keep traumatic thoughts and emotions from infecting people's conscious lives. However, defense mechanisms do not banish fearful thoughts but merely keep them hidden. If the defense mechanisms do not work, however, finding a good therapist may be necessary.

The Psychosexual Stages.   *Oral Stage (0–1).*   The earliest psychosexual stage begins at birth. From birth to about one year of age, gratification comes orally. Chewing,
biting, nursing, and eating become the sole forms of gratification. Babies innately respond to a mother's nipple, which becomes their first way to get their needs met. At
this stage babies often struggle, because their oral needs will not always be met.

Anal Stage (1–3).   At the anal stage, children have their first opportunity to exhibit
control and gain independence. While being toilet-trained, infants have the opportunity to release or withhold—their first control. Consequently, personality patterns become further molded at this stage of development. For example, an *anal explosive*
personality, defined by being messy and disorganized, may begin to develop and create a life-long pattern. Conversely, *anal retentive* people typically exert great control
open their own toileting behaviors early in life and continue as adults to be orderly,
controlled, and structured.

Phallic Stage (3–5).   The genital stage is characterized by a major shift in gratification.
Beginning sexual urges are the source of great fear. Children at this stage have many
difficult tasks to overcome and often their later problems in life germinate here. In the
genital stage, toddlers develop an attraction to their opposite-sex parent. This strong,
yet unconscious, desire becomes a well of difficulty. Little boys, attracted to their
mother, desire her, yet, someone much bigger and more powerful—Dad,— stands in
the way. This challenge, called the *Oedipus complex*, is difficult to resolve. The small and
physically weak toddler sees that his mother lacks a penis. The child fears that if he attempts to take over his mother, his father will remove the child's penis as well. The
child's belief creates an overwhelming *fear of castration*, and the toddler surpresses these
issues deep into his unconscious and begins to identify with his father as the safest way
to be close to mom. When they become aware of their physical lacking, female toddlers, too, have a great challenge as they develop *penis envy*. This envy, eliciting the
Electra complex, creates a great desire for father, but her mother stands in the way, so
the female toddler learns to identify with her.

Latency Stage (5–puberty).   The latency stage, existing until puberty, is characterized
by great repression of sexual urges. Children shove sexual energy deep into their unconscious minds and focus more on developing healthy same-sex relationships. Friend-
ships become their main source of enjoyment as motivation. This stage shows dormant
sexual behavior until the all-changing puberty arrives.

Genital Stage (Puberty–death).   The genital stage, focused on genital sexual gratification,
continues throughout life. Freud believed that sexual relationships with the opposite sex
begin at this stage and may lead to commitments such as marriage. Although not considered the most challenging stage of development, the genital stage is often plagued
with past repression and experiences. Earlier, unconscious experiences influence
choices and behaviors, often below a person's awareness. These experiences continue
to play out through adulthood.

Goals of Therapy. Freud's view of the mind serves as the basis for the goals of therapy. The structure and conflict that occur through the workings of the id, ego, and superego create a state of flux and movement. As a person attempts to surpress the primal drives of the id, the ego often struggles to mediate in a world of limited resources, which breeds psychological conflict. The superego that demands moral perfection puts great strain on the ego. This strain requires the ego to make decisions in a rational way while being tugged by two irrational components of the mind. Consequently, the main goal of psychoanalysis is understanding.

Ultimately the helper's goal is to move a client *through* past-repressed memories and mend or remove failing defense mechanisms. Problems of today are rooted in experiences in the past. Helping the client reexperience and move beyond past experiences is key to successful therapy. The unconscious, which houses all the deep thoughts and feelings, continues to be a person's greatest motivation of behavior. Yet, inherent in the structure of the mind, the unconscious is the part about which the least is known. Consequently much of the goal of therapy is to bring the unconscious forward; uncovering what is hidden becomes a paramount component of successful therapy.

Techniques. What would Freud do? Well, of course movies pan the inevitable. A client sprawled upon an antique fainting couch deep in thought speaks fluidly about mom and dad. This scenario is not inevitable but is often a component of therapy. Because the goal of therapy is to make the unconscious conscious, psychoanalytic therapists attempt to remove distractions and resistance allowing the client to *free associate*. This technique helps bring the depths of the unconscious forward. In addition, Freud utilized *dream analysis*, because it was, in his words, the "royal road to the unconscious." Finally, *interpretation* and *analysis of transference* (the client projects feelings through the therapist) further serve to bring the depths of consciousness forward. These crucial techniques require that the therapist knows when to appropriately interpret the client's feelings. This interpretation helps the client understand how current behavior relates to past conflicts and unconscious struggles (Corey, 2004).

Although often criticized for being a long-term therapy, psychoanalysis attempts to make long-term changes in clients. The integration of the mind and self-awareness are both a dynamic and worthy pursuit for moving the client. The techniques mentioned here allow both the therapist and client to see deep into the unconscious, which helps explain the client's current feelings, thoughts, and behaviors. As the client's understanding occurs, the therapist helps the client move forward, which contributes to long-term, meaningful change.

Freud and the Intentional Theory Selection Model. Obviously Freud was around long before the ITS model. In this historic highlight, Freud had presented *the* theory of psychotherapy. During the conception of Freud's work, no theories of helping competed with it. Other theories in existence at the time focused primarily on spiritual and biological issues, not on psychological ones. So, how would Freud's conceptualization look? At the base was his philosophy of life where he viewed humans as deterministic

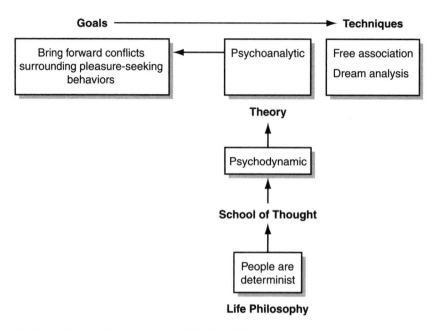

FIGURE 4.1   A Psychoanalytic ITS Model

and pleasure seeking. His school of thought was his own psychodynamic school and his theoretical orientation was his own psychoanalytic theory. And, through his own research, Freud developed his goals and techniques based on his philosophies. He wanted to help his clients, through such techniques as free association and dream analysis, understand how their deterministic nature and innate pleasure-seeking behaviors caused their presenting problems. Figure 4.1 shows the ITS model as it applys to Freud's theory.

Analytical Theory

A one-time student, mentee, and "adopted son" of Freud, Carl G. Jung offered an intuitively developed, creative and dynamic view of the psyche and human development called *analytical theory*. After a near, midlife breakdown, Jung emerged with a theory that showed that the truly healthy are not the young.

Life Philosophy.   Carl Jung believed that people are all holistic individuals connected at an ancestral level. He agreed with Freud that people possess physical drives. However, he believed that one's main life pursuit was to move intentionally towards *individuation*, which is a force that pushes us toward wholeness and helps *the self* to emerge. Although not historically designated as an existentialist, Jung felt that people longed for life meaning, and he identified humans as having a highly spiritual dimension.

Jung's view of humans was positive. He did acknowledge that peoples' past influenced who they were. However, he took a less-deterministic view of life that assumed people actively moved toward their potential. Consequently, Jung deemed that development occurs throughout the life span.

Jung offered a unique perspective of personality and is credited with coining the term *psyche*. Psyche is composed of three major systems: the ego, personal unconscious, and the ancestral, collective unconscious. The *ego*, peoples' current thoughts, feelings and reflections, is easy to access and contains their current experiences. Those emotions that people experience at the present time and information they are currently absorbing are housed in the ego, accessible and present. The *personal unconscious* houses those memories and thoughts that are filed away, accessible but more difficult to reach. If you imagine the face of your fourth-grade teacher, likely you accessed your personal unconscious. The teacher's face was likely accessible but was not at first present in your ego. Finally, at the deepest level and very difficult to access, is the *collective unconscious*. Through the study of myths, languages, and art, Jung realized that all cultures, from the most primitive to the most civilized, have common themes and stories. He found strong connections between cultures and identified a deeper, ancestral level to our psyche. He identified that deep within this ancestral level people contain *archetypes*, which are basic icons building their personality. For example, all people contain *shadow, the wise one, healer, anima* (our female side), *animus* (our male side), and *hero* images. When people have life experiences, they build upon these archetypes that formulate their personality. These archetypes serve as building blocks for categorizing and organizing experiences that ultimately make people who they are.

These archetypes, which are typically hidden from one's awareness, are expressed in dreams, religions, myths and cultural symbols. For example, take a Disney cartoon, a contemporary film, or any fable and decide who (or what) represents the hero and the shadow. Jung found that these symbols of collective unconscious could be found from the most contemporary of societies to the most primitive, removed tribes. Human connection serves to bind all people in some way while still allowing individual personality to emerge.

Jung, like Freud, believed that people are motivated by *libidinal energy*. However, later Jung opposed Freud's sexual and aggressive understanding of libido and perceived libido as creative life energy with a biological basis. This energy—moving back and forth, never lost or created, but placed in various areas of one's psyche—was constant movement. For example, people could place all of their energy in their creative, aggressive shadow side. Embracing their "evilness," people could entertain a life where they saw only negative in others and enjoyed controlling others though aggression. However, people could have energy fixated in their hero side where they are always looking for the hidden good in others while trying to care for them. Consequently, where people focus their libido drives their behavior and emotions.

Goals of Therapy.   Jung shared that a main goal of therapy is the integration of the psyche. Since he believed that people have a set and limited amount of psyche energy, then they must find balance in their psychological world and intentionally *assist their self* to emerge. This emerging self enables people to ultimately be full-functioning individuals. The main goal of counseling is *individuation*, or the integration of conscious and unconscious systems that is accomplished through insight, personality transformation, and even education (Kaufmann, 1979).

This individuation and emerging of the self is a lifelong, intentional journey. Unlike Freud, Jung believed that midlife is the first time an individual could begin to have integration, and he focused on the emerging of the psyche instead of the causes. As people grow, mature, and move toward individuation, they acknowledge and embrace all parts of themselves—the hero, anima, animus, healer and even shadow. Without this intention and integration, the true self could never emerge. Regarding individuation, Jung (1991) states:

> So although the objective psyche can only be conceived as a universal and uniform datum, which means that all men share the same primary, psychic condition, this objective psyche must nevertheless individuate itself if it is to become actualized for there is no other way in which it could express itself except through the individual human being (p. 179).

Techniques.   Jung did whatever it took for the client to gain insight, he was highly creative in therapy and believed in doing whatever was necessary for healing. However, first and foremost, Jung believed the analyst and client should have a warm relationship, which is the foundation of quality therapy. Egalitarian, respectful relationships are the core to therapy. He believed that only through these relationships would clients have the comfort to confess their stories and have the room to cathart. Although Jung was known to sing, pray, dance, utilize art, and even examine astrological charts, he is most known for two techniques—*dream analysis* and *archetypal analysis*.

Jung believed that dreams ultimately help people see the deepest layer of their unconscious. Through a process of self-understanding, people can strive, grow, and enhance. Additionally, as helpers, if you espouse a Jungian paradigm, you understand that clients reach for individuation and health as they gain a greater understanding of their psyche that can be best achieved through archetypal analysis.

Analysis helps to bring insight, which is the key to change. For example, we recently had a client about forty years old, who was struggling with assertiveness and presenting with marital difficulties. She shared the following dream:

> I was fighting with my husband, and he looked like me. I was trying to pull him in, almost into me. Not like I was going to eat him but . . . well, it sounds weird, because at the same time I was yelling at him and pushing him away, I was trying to hug him. He kept saying, "don't push me away, you need me." I didn't know what to do. I never really felt anger in the dream, but just fear or even guilt. I felt like it was wrong for me to hold on to him.

The client wisely believed the dream was a commentary on her marriage. She did push her husband away and yet wanted to draw nearer to him. However, to an analytic helper, the dream meant something more individual, a commentary on the client. As a midlife individual, her goal is integration and individuation. Her husband represented her animus—the male part of herself. Her goal of being assertive is hindered by the guilt and fear of embracing her more masculine (animus) side. The dream was telling her "you need" to integrate your animus and anima. Once she understood the dream, the client was much more able to be assertive without feeling guilt.

Individual Psychology

Another prodigy of Freud, Alfred Adler, also believed humans were motivated by a few basic needs and one in particular: socialization. Adler believed that the primary worth of all humans was rooted in Gemeinschaftsgefühl.

Life Philosophy. *Gemeinschaftsgefühl*, typically translated as *social interest*, is the core tenet of individual psychology. Adler became disenchanted with Freud's deterministic view that people are primarily sexual beings. Like Freud, Adler believed that one's primary personality was constructed and set at an early age. Consequently, he focused great energy on the development and role one plays in the family. Parenting style, sibling rivalry, and even childhood illness write the roles one will continue to play later in life. Parents who give too much, too little, or the wrong type of support may risk their child's ability to ultimately be a socially mature and useful person.

As reflected in the title of Adler's approach, people are holistic individuals (*indiviuum* is Latin for individual or whole). A major contrast to reductionism that Freud endorsed, this approach looks at the various components that make people human. Adler's concern was the entirety and completeness of the person.

Additionally, people are *teological* (goal-directed) creatures. All of one's actions, even the smallest, seemingly random action serves a purpose and can be understood when the goal is discovered. Adler believed that people have free will, free choice, and a *creative power* to choose their behaviors, consequently, they can choose new goals and behaviors. One's ultimate goal, *fictional finalism*, is the driving, yet unattainable goal. Our unattainable fictional finalism serves as all we strive to become. All people develop their own view of what they attempt to reach. People may have goals of perfection, goodness, being godlike, being the perfect father, the funniest person, and so on. These goals may guide their behavior but are immeasurable and ultimately unobtainable. For example, a boy may strive to be the perfect son. His behaviors along the way help him, as he views it, to make this happen. Although, this goal is immeasurable, striving to attain it drives his everyday behaviors.

As people strive to meet their life goals, they commonly develop smaller goals along the way to reach their fictional finalism. However, these smaller goals may not always be effective in other areas of their life. These *mistaken goals* lead people to make decisions that have emotional consequences. For example, if a boy is striving to become the perfect son, he may make the assumption that this goal requires him to always give of himself and not to meet his own personal needs. Consequently, at the extreme this goal will not work to bring him happiness. If he meets every situation believing that he must give, he may ultimately become drained and even resentful of others.

Adler believed innate to being born is a feeling of *inferiority*. People's natural beginning state is one where they feel "less than." However, this state is not a weakness or abnormality and serves truly to be a powerful motivation of human behavior. Due to their beginning stance, people strive to achieve superiority. This motivates them to achieve as they attempt to compensate for this feeling. If people do not develop ways to accomplish this, they run the risk of developing an *inferiority complex*, which includes a pervasive feeling of feeling less than others. An additional risk is the acquisition of a *superiority complex:* an attempt to overcompensate for one's own inferiority feelings with grandiose opinions of one's talents and success (Adler, Ansbacher, & Ansbacher, 1989).

In pursuit of the ultimate personal goal, Adler identified various *styles of life*, influenced by early experiences to help people along their goal-orientated journey. According to Adler, as social beings, people have several *life tasks* to accomplish. These tasks include *love, friendship, occupation, family,* and *spirituality.* Each of these tasks has unique social challenges. In this pursuit, the various styles of life drive how people are or are not successful in achieving them. The styles of life serve as the "spectacles" of how the person perceives his or her own life (Mosak, 1979, p. 44). Additionally, as part of people's style of life, they lean toward a personality type. *Dominant-type* people lack social interest and will often hurt themselves or others. Common *getting-type* people expect others to meet their needs and frequently become dependent upon others. *Avoiding-type* people minimize contact with others and the world, ultimately avoiding failure and success. These three types of individuals offer little to others, consistently struggle with problem solving, and have limited social interest. The fourth, and most healthy, style of life is the *socially useful type.* These individuals are able to accomplish the basic tasks of life while being socially minded. They typically contribute to the elevation of the human condition and society in general.

Goals of Therapy.   Adler believed that most of people's personality is established in the early years of their life. However, as creative individuals people do have the ability to change. Through insight, their perceptions change which in turn creates behavioral change. Because people are social creatures, increasing the social interest of clients is the ultimate goal of therapy.

Private logic—personal cognitive and emotional abilities—helps one in his or her pursuit of life goals. However, disruptive private logic, inferiority/superiority complexes, and mistaken goals all contribute to daily discouragement. Consequently, the goal of therapy is change—to reconfigure private logic, to gain healthy goals, to accomplish life tasks in socially useful ways.

Techniques.   Adlerian therapists first establish a therapeutic alliance: a relationship centered on warmth and collaboration. After establishing rapport, which is a necessary step for an Adlerian helper, a lifestyle assessment is required. Learning the client's family constellation including birth order, early recollections, private logic, and fictional finalism is key to client change. Lifestyle assessment is the key to the therapeutic process that assists the helper in learning about the client and later providing the client with insight and interventions.

The client's *constellation* represents the roles played within the family. These roles impact who the client is today. Understanding how people view their developmental years, tells the helper who they really are today. Adlerians also focus on gathering *early recollections*, a person's early memories. These recollections tell the helper much about the client's style of life and goals. The Adlerian helper believes that the important issue is not the reality and objectivity of early recollections but rather the client's subjective meaning that is revealed in early recollections. The roles clients play in their early recollections will likely continue to be played in their contemporary life. For example here are three early recollections. First when Anton was four, his kitten disappeared, never to return. Second, when he was five, his shoes were stolen by a big, mean neighbor kid. Third, when he was seven, his brother broke his favorite toy, a Star Wars Chewbacca doll. You likely see a theme. What do you think these say about Anton today? The recollections he shares about himself in the past, speak to who he is today. The Adlerian therapist would look at these early recollections and attempt to find patterns or themes. In this case, they might see that Anton felt hurt and loss in each of these situations; he felt like others were taking away what was then important to him. This, through an Adlerian perspective, would speak to whom he is today, suggesting that today, as an adult, he feels as though others unfairly take from him.

First, the Adlerian helper establishes rapport. Then, a thorough assessment occurs that includes gaining an understanding of the lifestyle, early recollections, birth order, family constellation, goals, and private logic. Thus, Adlerians have many therapeutic interventions to help the client in the change process.

Transactional Analysis

Want a nice warm fuzzy? I know where you can get one.

Eric Berne brought the historically popular transactional analysis (TA) to therapy sessions. We will explore strokes and games, and during this section, you may find a peer to give you a warm fuzzy to help you develop a new racket. Transactional analysis was made popular as an approach that laypersons as well as therapists could understand. Even though transactional analysis has lost the popularity it had following its inception, it is still a widely utilized therapeutic approach.

Philosophy. Transactional analysis may look a little familiar. Three *ego states*—one "id-ish" *child ego state*, one *adult ego state*, and one "superego-ish" *parent state*. Transactional analysis examines how each individual has three distinct, yet dynamic states and further looks at how these states influence how people interact with others. According to Berne, when people interact, or have *transactions*, they do so from one of three ego states that are a distinct way of feeling and thinking. Berne's "reconceptualization" of Freud's states describes social interactions (Day, 2004, p. 479). These ego states, seated separately in our brains, drive our thoughts, feelings, and actions. They motivate behavior and serve as tape recorders of our experiences. Each state serves its own unique purpose and arises as a way to interact with the environment helping people to get their needs met. These states contain *life scripts* that are based and formed during childhood as ways to survive.

The Child.   People's basic, yet creative child state plays their emotional powerhouse. When people react from the child state, they literally think, feel, and act as though they are children. The child ego state is comprised of two components. The *natural child* is that part of people that reacts with love, hate, playfulness, joy, anger, and impulsivity. It stores their basic, nearly innate emotions and releases them, nearly in raw form. The *adapted child* also has emotions that have been created by consequences of the environment. People's guilt, sadness, and regrets are all part of their adapted child that has learned there are consequences to the way they think, feel, and act. Through punishment and the reality of a world with limited resources, people learn to change or *adapt* to their environment. The natural child reacts to a chocolate cookie with joy, while the adapted child might feel punishment for having taken the cookie in the first place. The child is that part of people that is most emotional. Imagine how one might act at a serious event, such as a funeral or job interview, versus an unstructured event, like a professional wresting match. When people are excited, spontaneous, and emotional their natural child ego is in control.

The Adult.   The adult state is one's logical, Socratic self. In this state people are rational and separated from the affective world. When acting from this state, people serve as problem solvers, making decisions in a rational, calculated process. The adult state functions much like a mediator or computer that balances the emotional child and the rigid parent. The adult looks at logical constraints and attempts to make decisions while listening to but hopefully not being driven by the other ego states.

The Parent.   As people mature, they are given strong messages about how they should behave. As children they were told, "no," "be nice," "be seen and not heard," "always say please," "you must try harder," and "don't back down." Often passed down from parent and authority figures, these messages are many times placed deep in people's brains like VCR tapes to be accessed and played. The parent, comprised of the *critical* and *nurturing* parent, serves to be judgmental or supportive, respectively. When problem solving, the parent does not emote or think rationally, but plays an appropriate tape to drive actions. When confronted with a situation, the critical versus nurturing parent will react very differently. For example, if Kim's partner says, "I broke your favorite mug," her critical parent might say, "You should be more careful and think about others." However, if her nurturing parent is in control she might say, "I am glad you were honest with me because telling the truth is important."

As helpers you may expect some problems to occur, because the ego states, obviously, do not handle situations the same way. Anytime you react to clients with a specific ego state, they will react to you with an ego state.

One common difficulty is *contamination* that occurs when one ego state infuses into another and the boundaries become blurred. When this happens, people may think they are reacting as an adult, but they are truly acting as an emotional child that has contaminated the adult state. For example, if a person's child state has contaminated the adult state, and that person is denied a car loan, he may argue and even cry with the loan officer thinking his reactions are rational versus reacting as a logical adult.

Another common challenge occurs when one ego state becomes dominant and excludes the others. This *exclusion* serves as a great challenge, because each ego state is important and needed in certain situations. People who function primarily as a *natural child* will be quite emotional and likely make decisions this way. Consequently, they will not access those other paramount parts of themselves that are vital to every day functioning.

Every interaction between two people is a *transaction*. Every time you speak to someone, you are speaking from one ego state and speaking to another. For example, a therapist who wants a client to pay a bill may speak rationally as an adult ego to adult ego. She may question, "It has been awhile since you paid your bill, and our policy requires that bills be paid in 30 days. Do you need some extra time?" The client who was spoken to as an adult has the option to respond as an adult. If he does, they have a *parallel* or *complimentary* transaction—when a person responds from the ego state that was addressed. If however, her client responds to her as a *natural child*, the client may respond emotionally, while crying and say, "I have just been so busy, and nobody seems to understand." In this case they have a *crossed* transaction that disrupts communication. Finally, *covert* transactions occur when a person says one thing but truly means another. The therapist, sounding like an adult, might say to the client, "You should pay me so you don't feel guilty." Here the therapist sounds like she is speaking to the client's adult, but she is truly being deceptive and speaking to the client's child.

Goals of Therapy. Transactional analysis has several goals. One goal is to work on greater balance of personal ego states. Individuals who have contaminated or exclusive ego states will risk making unhealthy decisions. Each ego state is important and serves a function. Limiting ego states reduces an individual's ability to be responsible. Consequently, a major goal of therapy is to help clients understand and identify their ego states.

Because TA helpers have a focus on relationships, this approach is quite effective in group therapy (Gilliland & James, 1998) and is also utilized greatly in family therapy. All people have *life scripts* that alter how they view others and themselves. These scripts develop in childhood as a survival mechanism. Consequently, a goal of transacional analysis is to change these scripts. People's emotions and how they interact with others is greatly effected by whether they personally believe: (1) *I'm OK, you're OK;* (2) *I'm OK you're not OK,* (3) *I'm not OK, you're OK* or; (4) *I'm not OK, you're not OK.* Each of these scripts lends people to play specific *games* (a pattern of transactions) to obtain *strokes* (recognition from others) that often result in *rackets* (negative emotional consequences of games). People play games with others in attempts to obtain strokes. These powerful motivators are the basis of what people want from others and they will do nearly anything to obtain these strokes, even if they are negative. In TA therapy, a major driving goal is to help clients understand their own script, games, rackets, and transactional patterns so they can interact with others in new ways. These goals serve to help clients change patterns they have likely been playing since they were children.

Techniques.   Several techniques are utilized in TA therapy. First and foremost is *analysis.* Rational analysis, structural analysis of the individual, analysis of transaction, game analysis, and script analysis are key strategies (Gilliland & James, 1998). The power of transactional analysis is understanding. Consequently, the TA helper will use psychoeducation to teach clients the concepts and the vocabulary of transactional analysis that the clients must understand before beginning to apply them. In Thomas Harris's (1969) revolutionary book, *I'm OK–You're OK,* he advises the reader that in skipping the "method and vocabulary of transactional analysis" you would "not only miss the full significance . . . but would assuredly make erroneous conclusions" (p. 12). Consequently, the client must first learn the various definitions and then later learn to apply them to their life.

Additionally, transactional analysis is a *contractual* approach to helping. The client and helper set specific outcomes to assist the process of therapy. The helper works on an egalitarian level with the client and attempts to have a healthy working relationship based on trust. Through the therapeutic relationship, the helper will learn who the client is and begin to see the games the client commonly plays.

Because of this contractual approach, the client is active in choosing therapeutic goals and is empowered to help change occur. For most clients, however, the process of analysis will be by far the most therapeutic intervention. The games each client plays are often ingrained and immersed in life patterns. Clients are often unaware of the patterns and deeply ingrained ways they interact with others and build relationships. Through analysis, clients may for the first time understand how they react to others and why others react to them in the way they do. Analysis allows clients to see more clearly who they are and allows them the opportunity to begin to live a new way.

BEHAVIORAL SCHOOL OF THOUGHT

The behavioral approach takes a much different look at human behavior: Humans are shaped and determined by sociocultural conditioning. This view is basically one that is deterministic because all behaviors are believed to be a product of learning through conditioning and reinforcement. Both effective and ineffective behaviors are learned and typically are the result of learned or expected consequences. True, traditional behaviorists take a scientific, empirical approach and primarily focus on tangible behaviors, goals, and techniques.

Traditional behavioral thinking has many contemporary variations. The process of therapy still focuses on behavioral aspects of clients, but it does not ignore the need for emotional expression and a warm therapeutic relationship. For the purpose of example, only behavioral therapy will be introduced because this approach outlines the original philosophy of the behavioral school of thought.

Behavioral Therapy

B. F. Skinner (1948) in *Walden Two* describes a utopian society, where behavioral techniques are utilized to reduce the need for individual morality and make the need for personal value unnecessary. This revolutionary, controversial writing made practical the value of behavioral therapy. While the concept of utopian societies has little to do with today's counseling and psychotherapy, the work of B. F. Skinner does.

Philosophy.   Nearly everyday professionals and laypersons use techniques from behavioral therapy. Spanking, speeding tickets, gambling casinos, and even employee-of-the-month programs are all the results of several key behavioral theories. Behavioral therapists believe that people's behaviors are products of their environment, and their actions are the results of what happens to them. Behaviorists see people as genetic creatures. However, as empiricists, behaviorists believe people should only examine that which can be observed and measured. If something cannot be tasted, touched, felt, heard or seen, it is not key to therapy. Consequently, more value is placed on the present than on past experiences. Behaviorists are known for their adherence to the scientific method and objective approach to psychotherapy. An additional life view of the behaviorists is that we are all basically *hedonistic*—pleasure seeking. People seek reward and pleasure, while avoiding punishment and pain.

What causes emotional and behavioral problems in life? The same process that creates healthy emotions and behaviors creates problems—learning. Since *all* behavior is reinforced through the process of learning, both positive and negative behaviors and their respective consequences are learned. Each person is unique, and each has a unique learning history. The rewards people experience and the consequences (both good and bad) that they endure cause their behaviors.

Within traditional behavioral approaches, there are three major theoretical underpinnings that describe human behavior: *classical conditioning*, *operant conditioning*, and *social learning theory*.

Classical Conditioning.   Early in the twentieth century, while studying the digestive systems of dogs, Ivan Pavlov made an interesting discovery. He found that he could ring a bell and dogs would drool. The magnitude of his discovery forms the basis of many behavioral techniques and describes many basic human behaviors.

Pavlov showed that a stimulus that should not cause an automatic reaction could be made to do so. Pavlov rang his bell and gave his dogs food powder. What did they do? Salivate. He rang his bell again, gave the powder, and what did his dogs do? Salivate. Yet again, he rang his bell and gave the powder. What did the dogs do? You are correct. They salivated. Then, he again rang his bell without giving the dogs powder. What did the dogs do? Yes, again, they salivated. The powder was an *unconditional stimulus*—meaning it caused an automatic reaction, in this case drooling—the *unconditioned response*. When a neutral stimulus, like the bell, is repeatedly paired with an unconditional stimulus, like the powder, the bell becomes a conditional *stimulus* that can elicit a response—the *conditioned response*—on its own. Thus, learning occurs.

Operant Conditioning.   Although *classical conditioning* seemed to explain many behaviors, others (e.g. Bandura, Skinner) believed that there was more to learning. All behaviors have consequences, such as rewards and punishments that cause behavior. For example, if you make fun of someone's hair, that person may choose to kick you; pain is your consequence, and, you will likely no longer make fun. If teachers wanted to increase the amount of questions their students pose in classes, they could give a dollar to each student after he or she asked a question. An educated bet says that this practice would increase questions and class participation. *Operant conditioning* explains that every behavior is either promoted or not promoted by what follows.

Social Learning Theory.   Have you ever run your car over a cliff? If not, why? Have you received positive rewards, like money, for not going over a cliff? Then how did you learn not to? Social learning theory explains that people also learn vicariously by watching others. If you see a person get punished with a parking ticket for illegal parking, you can hopefully avoid learning the hard way by learning vicariously from others' mistakes.

Goals of Therapy.   In many ways, the goals of behavioral therapy are the most straightforward of contemporary psychotherapy approaches. Behavioral therapists spend their time with clients addressing specific behaviors that help their clients learn to behave differently. In this process, clients are often empowered to set specific goals that are relevant to them and their current presenting problem.

For therapy to be effective, data must be collected, goals must be set, and relevant interventions must be initiated. Finally, as an objective approach, behavioral therapy examines outcomes and strives to initiate assessments that are based on these interventions. The goals of therapy include helping clients change their environment, because environment is truly the cause of all behaviors, and reinforcing new, more effective behaviors.

Techniques.   Behavioral therapists utilize many techniques that are primarily based on classical conditioning, operant conditioning, and social learning theory. Techniques focus on changing the environment and behavioral consequences because all behaviors are fundamentally based on learning. The tool belt of a behavioral therapist is full and includes such tools as education, reinforcement scheduling, modeling, systematic desensitization, relaxation techniques, assertiveness and skills training, charting, contracts, aversion therapy, satiation, self-monitoring, and homework assignments (Corey, 2004; Day, 2004; Ivey, Gilliland & James, 1998; Ivey, & Simek-Downing, 1987). Behaviorists have been highly creative and have given the helping professions many tools to use, for example, *token economies.* This intervention is based on giving small rewards for positive behaviors that can later be traded in for larger awards. Additionally, behaviorists bring us *aversion therapy,* based on classical conditioning. A behavior can be limited by pairing it with something that is not enjoyable. For example, if you want to quit biting your nails, a helping professional might suggest you put extremely hot pepper seeds under your nails. Soon, biting will be associated with pain, and hopefully you will learn new behaviors.

A Behaviorist School Counselor and the Intentional Theory Selection Model.
For example, Jim a graduating therapist and school counselor believed, as do most behaviorists, that the key to changing a child's behavior is identifying target behaviors and changing reinforcements that perpetuate these behaviors. Jim commonly works with students who teachers have identified as "acting out." He has found that certain

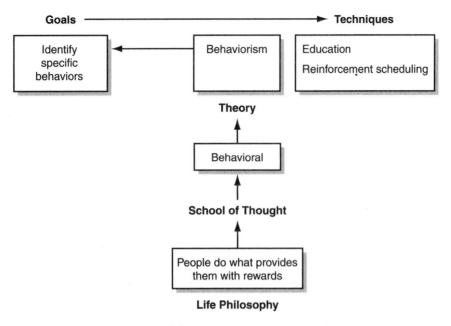

FIGURE 4.2 Jim's ITS Model

students, who behaviorally disturb the classroom environment, often get attention only when they act out. Consequently, Jim focuses on educating teachers about behavioral phenomenon and assists them in creating reinforcement schedules that reward students when they are on task and performing well in the classroom. Jim's ITS model might look like Figure 4.2.

HUMANISTIC SCHOOL OF THOUGHT

The core belief of the humanistic school is that humans have a basic inclination to become fully functioning. Individuals are viewed in a positive manner and the context of therapy is often focused on the affective world of the client, moving towards self-actualization, gaining trust, spontaneity, and focusing on the human condition. Humanistic approaches take a phenomenological, here-and-now approach. The relationship is thought to be fundamental to successful therapy and helping clients achieve their potential. The most common humanistic approaches are: *Client-centered, existential,* and *Gestalt.*

Client Centered

What do you think? What is at the core of client-centered therapy? Yes, the client. Client-centered (sometimes called Rogerian, person centered, or humanistic) typifies the humanistic approach and centers on the client as the center of therapeutic change.

Philosophy.   The true client-centered helper views the world and human nature as positive. People, left on their own volition, would reach their potential (Rogers, 1961). Humans strive towards *self-actualization* in a process of growth. Self-actualization, the process of moving towards one's greatest potential, is never achieved but is a continuous process. This actualization requires one to constantly grow and experience.

Client-centered helpers believe everyone is unique and everyone has a unique worldview. Consequently, clients should be understood in a *phenomenological* approach that requires the therapist to attempt to see the world as clients see the world. Although often hard to remember as a helper, the clients' emotions and actions make sense given the way they view the world. Carl Rogers (1995), often considered the father of humanistic therapy, stated it is important "to open one's spirit to what is going on *now*, and to discover in that present process whatever structure it appears to have" (p. 189). Rogers also believed that life and therapy is characterized by a subjective reality and should be immersed in the here and now. Each moment is unique and people are defined not by their past but by who they are in the moment.

Client-centered helpers believe that clients ultimately know themselves better than therapists could ever know them. Clients are experts on their own lives. Consequently, client-centered helpers may offer little advice and directives. They might be directive about the process of therapy, but they allow their clients to make their own choices. This approach serves many purposes, including empowering the client. However, the process component is even more important. For example, you could go to a therapist and ask what tie you should wear for a big interview; the answer given to you is the "power red tie." If you got the job, you might think it had more to do with the helper's choices than with your abilities. In contrast, if you did not get the job, you might be angry with the helper and feel you were led astray. A client-centered helper should help you find what you want and what ultimately works for you.

Goals of Therapy.   Ultimately, the major goal of therapy is to help the individual continue towards self-actualization. Unfortunately, at times life situations or your own perceptions may hinder your growth. The road to actualization can become blocked, and therapy is about removing these blocks. People have a natural tendency to move forward to reach their greatest potential, and they can surpass difficulties only through removing these blocks.

Does this mean people must have problems to be in therapy? No. Something will always be in the way towards reaching their potential. Therapy can focus on prevention or simply on helping someone become "more". Therapy is actually most effective for those who are relatively healthy as they have the energy, insight, and potential to learn.

A common block people often face is a distorted view of self (Gilliland & James, 1998). Consequently, through the process of therapy, helpers hope their clients can find greater self-understanding and increased congruence between one's *perceived self* and one's *real self*. This difference between who people believe they are and who they actually are causes great psychological turmoil and is a major roadblock to living out their greatest potential. If a workshop attendee gives speakers negative feedback about their presentation style, the speakers may believe, "they are bad public speakers," which may not be true. They may be great public speakers but view themselves based on this limited information. This view creates anxiety, and the job of the counselor is not to "directly reduce anxiety" but to increase congruence between the perceived and real self (Hazlar, 2003, p.166).

Techniques.   People are all individuals with different needs and wants. Therapy is immersed in phenomenology and the here and now. Consequently, directives and typical techniques are not commonplace in the client-centered approach. In contrast, the cornerstone of the client-centered approach is the therapeutic relationship. *Genuineness,* the ability to be *nonjudgmental,* and *empathy* are the keys to therapy and the therapeutic alliance. These three core conditions of therapy are *necessary* and *sufficient* for change to occur (Rogers, 1957).

Genuineness or the ability to be authentic requires helper transparency. Therapists must be aware of their own feelings and allow this awareness to be a part of the relationship. Clients know when therapists are being dishonest so developing facades only harms the therapeutic relationship. However, to be truly authentic is difficult, requires self-knowledge and understanding, and takes the ability to know and share one's self. These requirements challenge helpers in cognitive and emotional dimensions and also forces them to serve with congruence, being honest in both words and actions. This *congruence* challenges us, as it requires us to use ourselves as a therapeutic tool and reveal ourselves as individuals.

Being nonjudgmental or offering *unconditional positive regard* requires helpers to completely and wholly accept their clients, (Rogers, 1957). Therapists must not put conditions on therapeutic relationships in order for an environment of trust and acceptance to occur. They do not have to accept all that their clients do, but they must accept clients at the core for being human. To be truly effective, therapists must accept clients in their entirety.

Finally, for successful therapy, therapists must convey empathy to their clients. Empathy is first, the ability to see the world through the eyes of another, and second, the ability to convey this insight. This empathy requires that therapists take a phenomenological approach and truly listen to the affective world of their clients. A client-centered therapy requires such basic, yet truly powerful skills, as the ability to reflect the client's narrative, to listen, and to paraphrase all while producing rapport. As a helper understanding and having insight is important. However, to help clients move towards their potential, therapists must have the ability to share this insight with clients—to show them that they see their joys and struggles.

Existential

Why are we here? What happens when we die? What is our purpose? How can we live a meaningful life? These questions lie at the core of the existential approach. In this approach, the fundamental questions of existence are core to people's successes and challenges in life.

Philosophy.   Often known as philosophical helpers, the existentialists have woven their fabric into the tapestry of humanism. The existentialists are often misperceived as pessimistic, because they deal with such fundamental issues as death, isolation, anxiety, and questions of existence. They attempt to help clients deal with the fundamental and basic conditions of being human. For example, existentialists view life as ultimately meaningless (Yalom, 1995). Some people may see this view as discouraging or saddening, however, from an existential paradigm it offers them an opportunity to create their own life meaning and pursue their own life purpose. This belief allows people to make their life personal and to tailor their life's work to who they are.

Existentialists believe that ultimately anxieties and worries are consequences of basic and core conditions of life. People's most basic emotions stem from acknowledging the realities of life. For example, the fact that one will ultimately die creates great psychological stress. People question what death is like and what happens following it, and they may even imagine the world without them. This arena of unknown creates angst. People want to have answers to these difficult questions but often do not. Additionally, knowing that they will die reminds them that they are limited in the time they have to accomplish their goals. Death is a constant reminder that in order to do all they want, or to say all they want, people are working with an unknown timeframe.

Existentialists also acknowledge that people have complete freedom. However, this freedom frightens them, so they often pretend not to have it. For example, you might often like to sleep in. However, you *feel* you must go to work as opposed to sleeping in. You do not actually have to go because you have freedom. However, knowing that you are completely free can be scary. This realization challenges people's view of the securities they have.

Additionally, people struggle knowing that they are responsible and often fight accepting responsibility and look to blame others for any consequences. If people do not accept that they are the makers of their own situations, they run the risk of not taking control of their own life.

Several authors consider existential psychotherapy as more of a philosophical approach rather than a unique humanist approach (e.g., Corey, 2004). Existentialism serves as a way to view clients but is not a completely unique approach. Although existentialism has common identified tenets (Halbur, 2000), individual existentialists themselves are unique. Each individual is understood as unique, so it makes sense that there are as many existential approaches as there are existentialists.

Existential psychotherapy does not replace but builds upon humanism. Consequently, it is also present-focused, a phenomenological approach, holistic, believes in the uniqueness of others, and attempts to help others continue towards self-actualization. Rogers (1995) writes, "It is this tendency toward existential living which appears to me very evident in people who are involved in the process of the good life" (p. 189). He believed that a component of actualization is to live in an existential way.

Goals of Therapy.   Awareness is a major goal in existential psychotherapy (Corey, 2004). Like client-centered therapy, existenial psychotherapy focuses on moving forward and continuing towards actualization. However, existentialists also believe that their duty is to aid a process through which clients can confront conflicts and ultimate issues of existence, meaning, and what being human means (Hansen, Rossberg, &

Cramer, 1993). More specifically, this goal includes awareness of possibilities available, one's freedom to choose, responsibility for one's choices, and barriers to freedom.

However, another major goal in existential therapy is acceptance of the core conditions of being human. Helping clients to acknowledge their freedom and use it wisely is important. Accepting one's personal freedom is a much more difficult task than merely being aware. Acquiescence of responsibility is also key. Many clients have said, "I know I can do it." Yet, they do not follow through. To be active, to take control of one's self and one's life, is important. As a helper, you can serve to empower clients to make personal choices and to have the courage to follow through.

An additional and paramount goal of therapy is to help people find or create meaning in their behavior, their lives, and even their suffering (Frankl, 1967; Kottler & Brown, 1992). Accepting that life is meaningless is difficult, especially if people do not then take the next step to rediscover or create their life meaning. The existential helper will assist clients in discovering or rediscovering meaning in their lives.

Techniques. As was discussed in the client-centered approach, the helping relationship is necessary, and for the most part sufficient, for effective psychotherapy. This relationship continues to require the therapist's acceptance, authenticity, and empathy. Fundamentally, the therapist's task is to enter the client's world and understand the client's unique worldview (Corey, 2004; Kottler & Brown, 1992). Additionally, the counselor's role is to be present as clients confront their concerns rather than to be a problem solver (Corey, 2004) while helping clients accept responsibility for their own choices (Ivey, Ivey, & Simek-Downing, 1987). However, in general, existential counseling is not technique-oriented, it is relationship focused, and may utilize techniques from other supporting, counseling approaches.

An Existential Psychotherapist and the Intentional Theory Selection Model. John has consulted with Kristin, a psychotherapist who specializes in addictions. Kristin stated, "My clients drink, use, and abuse because it is all that fills voids in their life. Nothing else gives them meaning . . . It's like it's all they have to live for." Kristin also said that she had struggled finding a theory that worked for her. Additionally, she stated that, "people are free to make choices, good or bad." John asked Kristin to identify her goals with clients and she said, "to help them stop using drugs and alcohol and replace their use with more meaningful experiences." Based on this discussion John thought her ITS might look something like Figure 4.3.

Gestalt

Imagine, you take a large pan and fill it with tomato paste, garlic, basil, water, and some Italian sausage, add heat and stir. What you get is sauce, ready for your favorite pasta. Now, imagine you are given some carbon, oxygen, water, and sugar. What do you get? Confused. These ingredients are the components of which human beings are comprised. However, we are more then the sum of our parts—the mantra of Gestalt therapy.

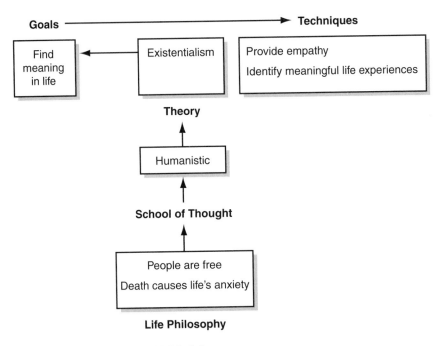

FIGURE 4.3   Kristin's ITS Model

Philosophy.   With strong roots in German philosophy and many parallels to the perceptual field of Gestalt psychology, Gestalt therapy is attributed to the work of Fritz Perls. The term *gestalt* means, a unified whole, and is the foundation of this humanistic approach.

Gestalt Psychology.   To understand the philosophy of Fritz Perls, you must first understand some basic assumptions of Gestalt psychology. Gestalt psychologists believe that individual components, such as the sugar in cola, have no meaning. Isolated parts are only meaningful when viewed holistically. Additionally, humans by nature attempt to bring about Gestalts—they attempt to organize data into complete wholes. Gestalt psychologists identified several key perceptual tendencies. One is the *principle of closure*. People's nature is to finish figures, to make sense of the data. Additionally, they tend to organize based on the *principle of proximity*. Items that are close together tend to be grouped together. For example what do you see in the following groupings?

O O O   O   O   O   O O O
O O O   O   O   O   O O O
O O O   O   O   O   O O O

Most individuals see a square made of circles in the first group, three columns of circles in the second, and three rows of circles in the third. This is due to people's desire to organize and make sense of data. In all three groupings the same amount of ink was used, but how you organized them changed. Another common way to organize data is through the *principle of similarity*. People have a strong perceptual tendency to group like objects together. For example, what do you see here?

```
O O O O X X X O O O O O O X X X O O O O
O O O X O O O X O O O O X O O O X O O O
O O X O O O O O X O O X O O O O O X O O
O X O O O O O O O X X O O O O O O O X O
X O O O O O O O O O O O O O O O O O O X
X O O O O O O O O O O O O O O O O O O X
```

Most people *do not* see rows of Os and Xs. Yet, that is what is typed. Likely they group the X's together and observe them as a wavy line.

Sometimes people organize data in very predictable ways. However, you must remember that each person is an individual and organizes data in different ways. Thus, each person lives in his or her own phenomenological world. Humans are limited to how much they can take in and can process. People constantly move their perceptual focus. What they focus on at anytime is called *figure* by Gestalt theorists. What grabs people's greatest attention, focus, or figure is highlighted in the rest of their perceptual field, referred to as *ground*. What do you see here?

```
O X O X
O X O X
O X O X
O X O X
```

Most individuals see one of two things, either rows of Os and Xs or alternating columns of Os and Xs. However, they really cannot see them both at once. People's ability to digest all information at the same time is limited.

Ultimately, several Gestalt psychology tenants become important in understanding Gestalt therapy. First, people actively attempt to organize and form wholes in their figure-ground field. Second, stimuli can be exchanged from ground to figure based on the phenomenological needs of the individual. Third, the individual's awareness of their surrounding field determines the accuracy of their perception (Perls, 1969b).

Gestalt Therapy.   If you have an understanding of the Gestaltist mind, you can start to understand Perls. Perls developed his approach based on the tenants of the psychologists. He believed, as a humanist, that people have one inherent goal—*self-actualization*. In this on-going process, at times people psychologically separate and lose their wholeness (Perls, 1969b). Similar to how they perceive, they emotionally can only focus on the *figure* and often lose site of the background.

Goals of Therapy.   The main goal of Gestalt therapy is to bring integration. A necessary goal for integration to occur is to gain awareness. People begin as whole individuals but at times loose their equilibrium. Helping the client gain a heightened self-awareness is the key for integration. Through awareness the individual can begin to complete gestalts.

Change requires that clients look at themselves and accept or reject what they will integrate. Consequently, a major goal of therapy is to assist clients in gaining a strong sense of self-responsibility. Only through responsibility can the client begin to integrate.

Techniques.   Basically, Perls wanted clients to gain awareness of who they are and who they are becoming. Consequently, in line with other humanists, he immersed himself and his clients in the here and now. The past is relevant as it brings one to today but is not the focus of therapy. Additionally, as each individual sees the world in a unique way, therapy, takes a phenomenological approach.

Perls (1969b) accessed a variety of techniques while believing that the helper should not be tied to technique. Many think that Perls gave more to techniques and methodology than he did to theory (Ivey, Ivey, & Simek-Morgan, 1997) and many of these techniques are utilized in various counseling approaches. The following are just a few examples.

Empty Chair.   Likely Perls' most famous technique, the empty-chair technique is utilized to help clients move beyond *unfinished business*—unresolved emotions. The counselor simply directs the client to imagine that someone is in the other chair and promotes the client to have dialogue with the imagined person. Often, the counselor will instruct the client to move to the other (empty) chair and play the various roles through. This powerful technique has found great application in working with couples and grief issues.

Pronouns.   Responsibility is key to effective change. Clients will often distance themselves from their own issues by referring to themselves in the third person or by using the word "you" instead of "I" in their narrative. The gestalt helper will promote clients to use personal pronouns such as "I" or "me" to aid in their personal growth.

Sharing Hunches.   The role of the counselor is not interpretation, but sharing hunches is a key technique. As the counselor stays present focused it is important to notice nonverbal messages. For example, the actions of a client who describes something as sad, while smiling and tapping a foot, likely has clinical significance. Sharing the potential meaning, or even asking the client to do so, can help the client gain greater awareness.

Dream Work.   Perls promoted the use of dreams in therapy. However, he was not looking for deep-rooted unconscious thought. Instead of traditional interpretation, he asked the client to play out specific roles or even to finish conversations begun in the dream.

These are just a few of the techniques available to you as a gestalt helper. These creative and diverse techniques serve to help the client through emotional impasses and continue towards self-actualization.

PRAGMATIC SCHOOL OF THOUGHT

In the family of pragmatic approaches, what people think and want is the root of their emotional and behavioral life. Consequently, a change in cognition or a realization of one's needs will inevitably cause a change in behaviors and emotions. Dysfunction and maladjustment are primarily problems of faulty or irrational thoughts. Therapy is often focused on learning what people need and want and understanding how their own thoughts and behaviors influence how successful they are in making this happen. The pragmatic helper often serves the role of teacher, helping clients learn how to help themselves.

Cognitive Behavioral

"I am good enough, smart enough, and doggonit . . . people like me." These famed words of *Saturday Night Live's* character Stuart Smalley exemplify the cognitive-behavioral approach. What people think about themselves and the world around them directly causes how they feel and behave.

Philosophy.   A contemporary and favored approach of managed care plans, is cognitive-behavioral therapy (CBT). Attributed primarily to Aaron Beck (1976, 1991), this approach, highly congruent with its title, views emotional and behavioral consequences as a result of inner thoughts and cognitions. Primarily, people control how they feel because of how they think. Typically, people feel that they are sad or happy due to what happens to them. "I won the lottery." "I am happy!" "I was late for work, I feel guilty." However, how people *view* their experiences is truly important not what happens to them.

Luckily, people are creative and highly imaginative and consequently have the ability to perform self-examination (Corey, 2004; Ivey, Ivey, & Simek-Downing, 1987). Consequently, the core emphasis of change must center on conscious thought (Hansen, Rossberg & Cramer, 1993). However, simple awareness of one's own thoughts and cognitions is not sufficient for change; ultimately, people must choose and want to live life differently (Ivey, Ivey, & Simek-Downing, 1987).

People's thoughts determine their emotions, and the meanings that they attach to events determine their reactions. Consequently, psychological distress (a fancy phrase for "bad feelings") is largely due to one's thought processes (Gilliland & James, 1998; Hansen, Rossberg, & Cramer, 1993). Unfortunately, people have a natural tendency to develop faulty, ineffective thinking. Therapy can be a powerful tool in positively influencing the lives of clients.

Goals of Therapy.   The ultimately goal of CBT is to teach clients to think about how they think so that they can correct faulty reasoning (Nelson-Jones, 2000). The greater goal is to assist clients to change systematic, faulty thinking and become able to be their own therapists (Nelson-Jones, 2000). As helpers, we are training clients to not need us and to be independent, autonomous human beings. Corey (2004) identifies the specific goals of CBT as: (1) helping clients identify and change maladaptive beliefs, (2) helping them test and evaluate their beliefs, and (3) helping them gain awareness of their automatic thoughts and change those that are maladaptive.

Techniques. In a cognitive-behavioral environment, therapy is largely psychoeducational and the emphasis is on developing practical skills for dealing with specific problems (Hansen, Rossberg, & Cramer, 1993). Cognitive behaviorists typically work collaboratively with clients and believe a mutual relationship with strong rapport is important in the process. In contrast to the client-centered approach, empathy, genuineness, and unconditional positive regard are considered *necessary* for change, but not *sufficient*. A therapeutic alliance is needed for change, but technique is needed as well.

Cognitive behaviorists contribute many techniques to the tool belts of contemporary psychotherapists. However, helpers are also willing to use the techniques from many other approaches—especially those of the behaviorists. For example, behavioral-modification contracting that is common in the behavioral approach is often utilized when this technique might help clients gain insight regarding personal cognitions.

However, some commonplace techniques used in this approach include: skills training, assertiveness training, relaxation techniques, and training in areas such as life skills, social skills, and communication (Corey, 2004; Gilliland & James, 1998; Ivey, D'Andrea, Ivey, & Simek-Morgan, 2002). Cognitive-behavioral therapy, as a directive, dynamic, and temporal approach uses any technique that can help clients to first identify automatic thoughts and then to change those that are maladaptive. Other techniques that help in this process include role-play, systematic desensitization, flooding, thought stopping, and cognitive modification.

Rational Emotive Behavioral Therapy

What type of a day have you had? Probably, you are really good at remembering what not-so-good events occurred today. Yes, you too likely fall victim to a natural human tendency—remembering the worst is easier than remembering the best.

Philosophy. Rational emotive behavioral therapy (REBT) believes that human nature fundamentally includes innate tendencies toward growth, actualization, and rationality as well as opposing tendencies toward irrationality and dysfunction (Ellis, 1962; Gilliand & James, 1998; Hansen, Rossberg & Cramer, 1993; Nelson-Jones, 2000). This polarization creates tension. Clearly events, facts, and behaviors play a role in one's daily health. However, one's beliefs about these objective events are more important than the actual events or behaviors (Gilliland & James, 1998; Ivey, Ivey, & Simek-Downing, 1987). Unfortunately, left to themselves, people have a tendency to move toward irrationality. Consequently, their own innate thoughts tend to move in such a way that negative thoughts thrive. Luckily, since all of people's behaviors and emotions are consequences of their internal self, they can change how they act and feel. However, they must attack their irrational thoughts.

With its initial development in the 1950s by Albert Ellis (1962), REBT purports that most people learn to think irrationally. Even interactions with parents influence and exaggerate the innate tendency to think in these irrational ways. Because people are developmental creatures, irrational thoughts become ingrained within their belief system at an early age and surface later in life (Gilliland & James, 1998). Luckily, humans are capable of change, and do so by changing their thoughts (Nelson-Jones,

2000). For example, here is Duane's experience with Penny. Even typing her name he feels a tinge of anger. In Duane's first year as a professor, he met Penny (named by him). He was in a hurry, a big hurry. He needed to get to campus, because he was being observed and evaluated in the classroom by a senior faculty member. With his nervous energy, he decided that he could not succeed without the aid of a cold soda, so he stopped at the local grocery. In front of him at the check-out line was Penny (you will see why she has been adorned with this name). Remember that Duane is in a hurry. Penny said, "It is a good day to use the change in my purse." So, in order to pay her $8.93, she rummaged through her palatial purse looking for every last penny (thus her adorned name). Duane was getting angry, very angry. As Penny counted out her last penny, she had only $7.53. At this point, Duane began to personally understand rage when Penny took the next three minutes writing a check for $1.40. He was so angry— but, why? He was angry because of two major irrational thoughts. First, he believed, "I might be late for my observation, I will then be fired and forced to never eat again." Second, he believed, "my time is more important than Penny's." These irrational thoughts caused him to enter campus (which he did make on time) sweating, angry and anxious. Who was at fault? Not Penny, but Duane.

Goals of Therapy. The primary focus of REBT is to change the way people think, as thoughts rather than events, cause emotional problems (Gilliland & James, 1998; Kottler & Brown, 1992). Consequently, the main goal of REBT is to reduce self-defeating, irrational thinking (Gilliland & James, 1998).

The goals and process of REBT are often summarized using the *ABC method. A* refers to the activating event or adversity. *B* is the individual's beliefs about the event, which may be rational and helpful or irrational and maladaptive. Finally, *C* refers to the emotional and behavioral consequences of those beliefs. The working goal of the therapist rests in disputing those irrational beliefs, *D*, and helping the client obtain more rational, helpful beliefs. If successful, clients gain new behavioral and emotional consequences symbolized by *E*—a new, more effective view (Gilliland & James, 1998; Nelson-Jones, 2000).

Fundamentally, REBT attempts to change the client's basic value system (Hansen, Rossberg & Cramer, 1993) and the ultimate consequence is for the client to "not just feel better but get better" (Nelson-Jones, 2000, p. 200). As is common in other cognitive-behavioral approaches, the therapist attempts to help the clients "become their own therapists" (Nelson-Jones, 2000, p. 201) so that they may live a rational life, free from the therapist.

Techniques. It is common for REBT counselors to convey unconditional acceptance. However a warm relationship is not considered necessary, and certainly not sufficient, to effect change. Conversely, too much warmth may actually lead to client's dependence and approval seeking and thus hinder client growth (Gilliland & James, 1998; Nelson-Jones, 2000). Some REBT counselors believe that the relationship between counselor and client is important initially (Hansen, Rossberg & Cramer, 1993). Consequently, since the relationship is not the focus, techniques are. The most common technique is to teach. Helpers teach their clients about REBT assumptions and how the consequences of human nature play out in their lives. Helpers focus on teaching clients how to think differently.

One technique common to the process of REBT is confrontation (Ivey, Ivey, & Simek-Downing, 1987; Kottler & Brown, 1992; Nelson-Jones, 2000). However, a wide variety of techniques are used in REBT therapy to help clients identify and change beliefs. Some techniques such as disputing irrational beliefs and bibliotherapy work primarily in the cognitive arena. However, affective and behavioral aspects are also addressed and techniques might include imagery, role-playing, homework assignments, and skill training (Gilliland & James, 1998; Nelson-Jones, 2000).

Reality Therapy

People would love to constantly have every one of their needs met to complete satiation. However, one big, ever present force stands in the way—reality.

Philosophy.   Human beings strive to have their needs meet. According to helpers who use reality therapy, human needs fall into five major areas: to survive, to love and be loved, to have power, to have freedom, and to have fun. To *survive* requires that people have food, water, shelter, and safety. Additionally, they have the basic need to *belong*, to give love to others, and receive love. People need to feel close to others and to feel others need and want them. Although the needs to survive and to love are important, people have other needs as well. To be playful, have *fun* and be active in recreation are important to the human mind. Additionally, people have the need for control and *power* and *freedom*. These needs define what it means to be human (Glasser, 1998). Our behaviors are our tools to getting our needs meet.

However, the founder of reality therapy, William Glasser (1998), shares that getting one's needs met is not always possible. People consistently seek to have their needs met in a world where resources are limited and they cannot consistently have all their needs met completely. For example, if people consistently work to have their power needs met by taking control of others, telling others what to do, and by just being bossy in general, they will likely not get others needs meet. For example, meeting the need for power would likely hinder one's ability to give and receive love.

The effectiveness of human beings is ultimately based in their decisions. Most every scenario presents people with choices, and their ability to make choices that meet their basic needs determines their level of health. On one side of a continuum are those who can meet their needs in socially appropriate ways versus those who cannot.

Unfortunately, learning to get one's needs met is not a guarantee that they will be met. Children learn that the best way to get food is to cry. If an infant's stomach was empty due to lack of food, he or she would cry, and the parents would inevitably take care of the infant's needs. Crying worked. Now, if adults tried that same approach in a meeting, they would likely be met with some strange stares. A reality therapist would assist them in learning what their fundamental needs are and effective ways to get them met.

Goals of Therapy.   The primary goal of reality therapy is to help clients make effective choices, which requires the assistance of the helper in this process. A necessary goal of therapy is helping the client accept responsibility. Making choices requires that clients accept their own role in making change (Glasser, 1965). Often, clients want change but do not want to do the work. They must realize what their own role is in creating change.

Understanding is also a driving goal. The helper must assist clients in understanding their own needs. What do the clients want? For most, the basic answer to this question is "something different." However, each individual has different desires within the basic human needs. Identifying these needs is crucial to making new choices.

Techniques.   How can counselors help? First, they must form a relationship with clients. An effective working relationship requires a helper who offers the client support. Additionally, the helper should be nonjudgmental. As a helper, you will likely have different needs and make different choices than your clients. First, you must understand that your clients' choices make sense to them. They believe their decisions are the best way for them to get their needs met. At some point, their behaviors were rewarded, but they just are no longer working.

Reality therapists do, however, have several signature techniques. First, they will often use *contracts* and *plans* with clients, which helps clients articulate specifically what they plan to do to make changes in their lives. Another common technique is termed *pinning down*, which is an essential process helping the client be specific in when and how they will follow through with a plan. For example, if Kim asks Duane to "contact the accountant for our private practice" he will respond with, "I will." However, she is wise, and knows Duane will never do it if that is his response. As an individual seated in reality, she then asks, "When?" She is following the principles of reality therapy. For example, if a client shares that they will start taking medicine, as a helper, you may explore when, with what doctor, and even how it will be financed.

An additional reality strategy is to promote clients adopting *positive-addicting behaviors*. Positive-addicting behaviors are those that are so important in people's lives that without them they feel a void. Prayer, meditation, exercise, helping others, and volunteering are all examples of behaviors that serve people in socially appropriate ways and that fill voids in their lives and become meaningful to them. Clients who are successful in achieving positive-addicting behaviors are more resilient to challenges when they are faced with them. Positive-addicting behaviors serve to provide clients with greater tolerance when they are faced with situations that cause basic needs to be challenged (Glasser, 1965).

Reality, Being a Student and the Intentional Theory Selection Model.   A graduate student in psychology came to Kim complaining of feeling "depressed and burned out." He complained that all he did was study and work. He was feeling "out of balance" and that life was "not giving him what he wanted." He came in for several sessions, and then on the fourth session, he came in smiling, saying he had "figured it out." He described that after reading a chapter on reality therapy, he was not making

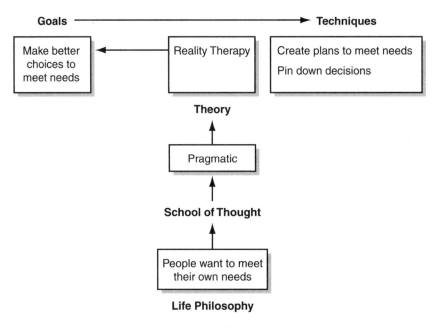

FIGURE 4.4   A Graduate Student's ITS Model

"good choices" in meeting his life "needs and wants." He said, "I have forgotten to play." His ITS would include his life philosophy of "people struggle to meet all of their needs and wants" and that "people need fun" (see Figure 4.4).

CONTEMPORARY SCHOOL OF THOUGHT

As information and research on counseling is collected, new helping theories emerge. These approaches often include aspects of previously founded theories. Currently, contemporary approaches tend to be heavily focused on phenomenology, human uniqueness, multicultural concerns, and client empowerment. The contemporary approaches we present are not always theories that stand on their own in a therapy session, but rather paradigms that may be incorporated into existing theories. Additionally, inherent in the contemporary approaches are the common themes of advocacy and prevention.

At one level, having contemporary approaches serve as a school of thought may seem like a "cop out." The theories incorporated in this school do not fit smoothly into the aforementioned schools and consequently are placed together. However, their placement together serves the field because these approaches may not fit well in to traditional schools, but they are worthy approaches deserving attention and may meet the needs of the changing demographics of clients served by counseling and psychotherapy. These valuable approaches to counseling and psychotherapy are not included in the Intentional Theory Sorter (ITS). The exclusion of the theories is not based on their merits, but rather on the fact that they are integrative and/or eclectic in their approach to therapy. The purpose of the ITS is for burgeoning therapists to first become grounded in one or two specific theories before they branch out into eclectic or integrative approaches. Thus, the theories categorized in this school are multicultural counseling and therapy (MCT), feminist theory, narrative, and solution-focused, brief therapy. Each of these theories will be described individually, following the format of previous theories within each school of thought.

Multicultural Counseling and Therapy (MCT)

Often presented as a unique and independent approach, multicultural counseling and therapy is a contemporary answer to working in diverse world, however, it can be utilized as a separate theory or may be incorporated into existing theories (Corey, 2004). Being aware of multicultural issues is important in the counseling relationship. However, it is not only important to focus on clients' individual values and beliefs but the therapist's as well.

Philosophy. The need for multicultural counseling and therapy arises from the Western-European basis of many theories of counseling and psychotherapy (Sue & Sue, 2003). Clients from minority groups may not share the worldview inherent in many traditional theories. Thus, culture must be examined in the counseling and psychotherapy realm (Sue & Sue, 2003), because cultures serve as a strong building block to who clients were, are, and become. "All learning is culturally defined and comprehended" (Pederson & Ivey, 1993, p. 26) as is one's own identity. Consequently, multicultural helpers frequently address specific dimensions of culture, including power distance, degree of individualism or collectivism, levels of uncertainty avoidance, trust and mistrust, and masculinity and femininity (Pedersen, Draguns, Lonner, & Trimble, 1996; Sue & Sue, 2003).

Multicultural helpers value the importance of cultural identity and its development (Ivey, Ivey, & Simek-Downing, 1987; Pedersen et al., 1996) and believe that ethnicity is an important aspect of meaning in personal belief systems (Nichols & Schwartz, 2001). Consequently, the development of the MCT approach was spawned by the critique that some mainstream theories propose too individualistic worldviews (Pedersen et al., 1996).

Fundamentally, counselors who incorporate the MCT approach into their clinical repertoire firmly believe that the presence of an alternative worldview, background, or culture does not necessarily indicate pathology (Nichols & Schwarts, 2001). Further, culturally competent counselors are aware that problems, concerns, and communication patterns may differ across cultures, and they are skilled at recognizing and treating culture-bound disorders (Pedersen et. al., 1996; Sue & Sue, 2003). Consequently, problems may be external rather than internal to the client. For example, the problem might be racism in society (Ivey, Ivey, & Simek-Downing, 1987) versus an individual being "pathological" or paranoid.

Goals of Therapy.   A culturally competent therapist has the awareness, skills, and knowledge of cultural issues and their intersection in the therapeutic process. Often, the first and foremost goal of multicultural counseling is cultural awareness. Effective multicultural helpers are aware of their own cultural values and biases and how they may be detrimental to the counseling relationship (Gilliland & James, 1998; Pedersen & Ivey, 1993; Sue & Sue, 2003). Therefore, pluralist-minded therapists not only strive to understand their clients' worldviews but must also have a consistent, life goal of self-understanding. In addition, helpers must have an understanding of how their own cultural identity adds complexity to the therapeutic relationship. Additionally, therapists with cultural awareness view dissimilarities between themselves and their clients as comfortable differences, not deficits (Sue & Sue, 2003).

Culturally competent counselors possess knowledge of worldviews other than their own (Sue & Sue, 2003). The goal of awareness is complicated because counselor interventions are based upon knowledge of the specific culture of the client and institutional barriers that might affect the client (Pedersen & Ivey, 1993). Being knowledgeable about cultures other than one's own may entail what is called "cultural role taking" whereby the therapist "acquires practical knowledge concerning the score and nature of the client's cultural background, daily living experience, hopes, fears, and aspirations" (Sue & Sue, 2003, p. 20). Inherent in the process of cultural role taking is an understanding of the sociopolitical influences and institutional barriers in the lives of clients from diverse backgrounds (Sue & Sue, 2003).

In addition to awareness and knowledge, appropriate and effective skills and interventions are necessary components of multicultural counseling and therapy (MCT). Culturally competent counselors must have the ability to generate both verbal and nonverbal communication because of the various ways diverse groups may value communication (Sue & Sue, 2003). For example, in some Native American cultures families share their stories and history through storytelling. This norm may alter how a therapist gathers information from a client of this culture. In addition to being able to communicate in a variety of ways, culturally competent counselors may need to play various roles within the counseling realm. Some roles may include that of consultant and advocate as the clients' needs dictate.

This approach, consequently, has implications that move beyond the therapy hour. Multicultural counselors often work to change oppressive systems (Pedersen & Ivey, 1993). Thus, counselors may serve as advocates not only initiating client change but also reaching out on political and sociological levels.

Techniques.   A major technique in the MCT approach centers on the role of the counselor who must consistently consider the client's worldview, background, and culture (Ivey, Ivey, & Simek-Downing, 1987; Pedersen, Draguns, Lonner, & Trimble, 1996). Consequently, effective counseling requires that counselors be aware of how their skills and interventions might be perceived differently by different groups of people (Ivey, Ivey, & Simek-Downing, 1987; Pedersen & Ivey, 1993). Counseling skills and techniques are often appropriate only to specific populations, thus, the helper has the difficult job of anticipating how a specific technique will affect a client.

Additionally, a multicultural counselor must be a wise consumer of previous research and remember that many interventions "proven" to work have had limited testing in certain populations. Counselors must maintain flexibility and work to reframe or revise definitions of basic concepts such as empathy, health, and growth (Pedersen, Draguns, Lonner, & Trimble, 1996). They may even need to modify or vary techniques that will more effectively address clients of various cultural backgrounds (Pedersen, Draguns, Lonner, & Trimble, 1996; Pedersen & Ivey, 1993). Effective helpers do not have to "throw out" their own personal theory or techniques that previously they have used effectively. Effective counselors do, while gauging their own worldview and that of their clients, need to be culturally appropriate in meeting the clients' needs. This difficult task is key to effective multicultural counseling and psychotherapy.

Feminist Theory

Feminist theory is not unique to the field of counseling and can be found in the fields of philosophy and gender studies, as well as art, film, literature, and many others. However, feminist theory emphasizes empowerment and advocacy and is increasingly becoming integrated within the helping professions.

Philosophy.   Like the multicultural approach to counseling and psychotherapy, feminist theory can stand as a unique theory but is often integrated into other theoretical approaches. Feminist theory examines oppressive sociological trends and how they relate to defined problems and pathology of women. Additionally, this approach has a variety of beliefs that are often categorized as radical, liberal, social, and cultural (Enns, 1993). However, a common belief of feminist helpers is that our established patriarchal systems subjugate women and either create or support the psychological and sociological challenges women face (Corey, 2004; Ivey, Ivey, & Simek-Downing, 1987; Nichols & Schwartz, 2001).

Feminist therapists focus on the implications of gender issues (Nichols & Schwartz, 2001) and shed light on the importance of reproductive and biological issues that play roles in women's lives as well as the all too common issue of violence. Additionally, feminist theory strives to maintain a positive attitude toward women (Corey, 2004) and views the characteristics of connection and caring as strengths versus weaknesses. Feminist theory deems that problems tend to lie in the social-cultural context, specifically in a patriarchal society (Corey, 2004; Ivey, Ivey, & Simek-Downing, 1987; Nichols & Schwartz, 2001). The theory deems that external forces such as oppression, discrimination, and harassment may be the source of many disorders and psychological stress, versus a client's internal shortcomings. Thus, the therapist must understand that client concerns do not happen in isolation.

Goals of Therapy.   The main goal of feminist theory is to help clients see the world in a variety of ways and provide them with choices that will allow them to live authentically (Enns, 1993; Ivey, D'Andrea, Ivey, & Simek-Mogan, 2002; Mancoske, Standifer, & Cauley, 1994; Matsuyuki, 1998). Additionally, a driving goal of feminist therapy is to deconstruct traditional patriarchal culture and to establish and strengthen egalitarian, women-supported roles (Corey, 2004). In this pursuit, feminist helpers also strive to encourage and support interdependence (Ivey, Ivey, & Simek-Downing, 1987) as opposed to the goal of independence found in more traditional, historical approaches. In this process, feminist helpers strive to give women alternatives to the roles they play (Mancoske, Standifer, & Cauley, 1994).

Techniques.   As the basis of the counseling process, the feminist therapist must form an egalitarian relationship with the client. However important this relationship may be, the feminist therapist also actively utilizes community resources, participates in therapy, gives information, and provides personal validation (Ivey, Ivey, & Simek-Downing, 1987). In general, counselors have a similar and necessary repertoire of skills across the various theoretical approaches. However, the feminist helper must also strive to listen attentively, honor their clients, challenge stereotypes, and support equality (Corey, 2004).

Feminist helpers typically serve in a collaborative role and strive to validate clients and support the development of women within society (Corey, 2004; Ivey, Ivey, & Simek-Downing, 1987). As a political and social approach, like the MCT approach, counselors move beyond the therapy hour, often striving to make larger changes. Feminist theory is based in part on the notion that "the personal is political" and that oppression occurs in many forms. The theory deems that external forces such as oppression, discrimination, and harassment rather than a client's internal deficiencies may be the source of many disorders and psychological stress. Thus, examining and evaluating social structures and biases is often a technique during therapy (Nichols & Schwartz, 2001) as is raising consciousness about difficulties that may be due to prescribed gender roles. Therapy may also include taking action to eliminate injustice rather than adjusting to the world as it is (Ivey, Ivey, & Simek-Downing, 1987).

To complicate matters, techniques greatly vary depending on which style of therapy is used. For example in liberal, feminist therapy, the focus is often to "minimize the differences between men and women and to assume that within bias-free environments, men and women will behave similarly" (Enns, 1993, p. 45). However, a cultural feminist would attempt to "emphasize differences between men and women and place special importance on the development of nurturing, cooperative, interpersonal qualities within society" (Enns, 1993, p. 46). Although the various styles of feminist therapy rely on unique techniques, their emphasis is common.

Feminist Theory and the Intentional Theory Selection Model.   The ITS of a feminist may look unique as he or she may utilize various techniques to meet the major goals of this philosophical approach. For example, a feminist therapist with whom Kim recently talked shared that he believes that many of his clients with eating disorders struggle due to "society norms of what is attractive." He believed that his clients struggle to meet media and sociological icons but, obviously, fail as these icons are not typically realistic. Consequently, many of his clients struggle not just with unhealthy eating behaviors but also with issues of self-esteem. He articulated what his ITS might look like (see Figure 4.5).

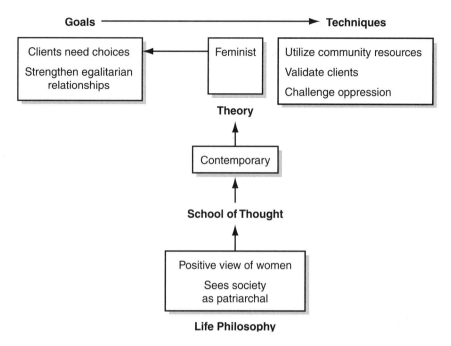

FIGURE 4.5   A Feminist's ITS Model

Narrative Counseling

Narrative therapy and its contemporary popularity is attributed primarily to the work of Michael White. When we first heard of narrative therapy, it made us think of someone reading bedtime stories to us. And, to be quite honest, that sounded pretty good. We were partially correct, narrative helpers do focus on the stories their clients tell.

Philosophy.   Ultimately, narrative helpers believe that as individuals people make sense of their everyday lives through narratives (Rosen & Kuehlwein, 1996; Russell, Van de Brock, Adams, Rosenberger, & Essig, 1993). These stories include what people want, what they like about themselves, and even what they want to change. How they define themselves is fundamentally through the stories they share. People may share stories of themselves as a son, daughter, parent, partner, and so on. The stories they choose to tell say much about who they are.

Narrative therapists also believe that people are social creatures and that much of what they describe as paramount in their narratives occurs within relationships. Consequently, therapists must understand clients in a social context. Narrative therapists believe that personal experience is ambiguous and may be understood and interpreted in multiple ways, and they believe that the stories people tell themselves are important in determining how they will act (Nichols & Schwartz, 2001).

Additionally, narrative helpers take a positive view of humans, tend to see the best in people, and typically believe that people have good intentions (Nichols &

Schwartz, 2001) and strive to live in a "good" way. Of course, this approach is subjective; there is no right and wrong, good and bad, and especially normal and abnormal.

Philosophically, narrative helpers are social constructivists who believe people are greatly influenced by their culture and environment. Additionally, narrative theorists believe that the truth of experience is created rather than discovered (Nichols & Schwartz, 2001) and consequently believe truly understanding others requires seeing how others view the past, present, and future (Nichols & Schwartz, 2001; Zimmerman & Dickerson, 1996).

Goals of Therapy.   The goal of narrative therapy is not just problem solving but is an attempt to change the client's whole way of thinking and living (Nichols & Schwartz, 2001). Problems are external to the individual and problems occur consistently. The therapist must help the individual be prepared not simply offer a therapeutic bandage for the current pain the client faces.

People tell others and themselves who they are through stories of their own lives and experiences. The stories help define where they have been and what they have done to produce who they are. If you tell someone who you are by sharing stories of glory, you define yourself as confident. If you instead tell someone who you are by your defeats, you share a person of failure. As helpers, you cannot change the past, but you can help clients *restory* or tell their life story in a new way.

As people develop, each has experiences that shape their stories. For example, when Duane was five he started wearing glasses and he also won his first award, most creative, fire-safety poster. When he was twelve, he was picked on by a few boys for wearing the wrong shoes, and he was given an award for outstanding computer skills. Each of these events had a personal, subjective meaning attached to it for Duane. If he entered therapy and said, "I feel like a successful person," which events do you think he used to define himself? Likely, he would describe himself through successes: he won awards when he was five and twelve. However, if he entered therapy and said, "I am different," he likely defined himself by those experiences that separated him: wearing big glasses and funny shoes. If he entered therapy, defining himself as *different*, your goal may likely be to help him restory and define himself as *successful*.

Techniques.   The narrative therapist serves as a collaborator. Like a driver education instructor, the therapist is along for the ride and may even give directions, but the client has a hold of the wheel. In this process, the counselor is active, often asking many questions to aid in the client's understanding. Additionally, the therapist is active in discovering and articulating client strengths, often looking for exceptions in the client's story. *Exceptions* occur when the clients shares experiences that are contrary to how they are defining their story. For example, if a client describes himself as being unassertive but then shares a time he stood up to someone, the therapist sees an exception. By identifying this exception for the client, the therapist can help him begin to see himself in a new way.

Some write that the basic goals of narrative counseling are to increase clients' choices, to coauthor new stories while helping clients view themselves in a new way, and to transform clients' identity (e.g., Nichols & Schwartz, 2001). In this process the helper must develop an initial narrative that externalizes and personifies the problem, seek unique outcomes, deconstruct the story, develop a new story or life narrative, and reinforce the client's new story (Corey, 2004; Nichols & Schwartz, 2001). However, narrative therapists often considered *externalization* the most important technique they use (Rosen & Kuehlwein, 1996; Weist, Wong, Brotherton, & Cervantes, 2001). Effective narrative therapists help their clients to see that their problems exist outside of themselves (Corey, 2004; Nichols & Schwartz, 2001), which allows clients to be separated from their problems, instead of defined by them. Additionally, this approach "allows conflict to decrease, lessens the sense of failure, encourages the client to struggle against the problem, opens new possibilities, and creates dialogue" (Weist, Wong, Brotherton, & Cervantes, 2001, p. 5).

Of course, an additional major technique of the narrative helper is to promote storytelling which, for many people, is therapeutic in and of itself; clients gain relief through their own sharing. However, for other clients, storytelling is simply a necessary step to begin doing therapeutic work (Rosen & Kuehlwein, 1996) that often includes the use of metaphors as a powerful tool. Ultimately, the client should end therapy with a new story, a story defining self in a positive, healthy ways.

Solution-Focused Brief Therapy

In the days of Freud, therapy was often five times a week, for many years. How would this settle with your insurance company? Solution-focused brief therapy takes the assumption that change can be facilitated effectively and quickly.

Philosophy   Solution-focused brief therapy with its many different names and diverse founders (e.g., Berg, 2003; de Shazer, 1985) is becoming vastly popular as a time-sensitive approach. Helpers practicing in this paradigm believe that specific changes can occur in a brief time, when the time is focused. In day one of therapy, the solution-focused helper gathers information from clients to learn what changes they want to have occur. Solution-orientated helpers speak little on the etiology of problems. The focus of solution-oriented approaches is defining the problem, not why it exists.

One of the best descriptions comes from Gilliland and James (1998) who state that solution-focused therapy can be described as, "a person-centered, behavioral stew with a dash of cognitive-behaviorism thrown in for good measure" (p. 309). Helpers in this paradigm do not direct their clients into making change that is valued by the therapist. Instead, staying future focused, the helper assists clients in finding those areas that they want changed.

Similar to the humanistic approaches, solution-focused helpers understand that their worldview is different from their clients' view. A client's behaviors and emotions truly only make sense from an individual, unique perspective. Consequently, a phenomenological approach is key to therapy.

Solution-focused helpers believe that one key component of therapy is to first determine what an individual is doing that is contributing to the problem. Often, clients do not realize, or do not articulate, what they do to actively make their problem or problems continue. This vital component of therapy is often the first question solution-focused helpers try to answer.

A second belief is that knowing where one wants to go makes getting there much more likely. People can easily get lost if they do not know their destination. The solution-focused helper first helps clients realize where they want to go because without that knowledge, direction cannot be found.

Goals of Therapy.   Quite simply, the paramount goal of solution-focused brief therapy is to eliminate problems. Actually, little more needs to be stated regarding the goals of therapy. Only fix what needs fixing. In solution work, the goal is to see what needs to change for the specific client and then to make that happen. Consequently, therapy is focused and specific about what change needs to occur.

Techniques.   Imagine that this book is magic and after reading it you would be the therapist you always wanted to be. Knowing what would happen, how would you be different then you are today? This variation of the *miracle question* typifies a paramount technique in the solution-focused approach. The question moves immediately to seeing what the client wants different. The miracle question is often asked the first day in therapy, because it helps clients move to a future orientation where their problems have changed and hopefully disappeared. "If I could give you a magic pill that would change your life to be exactly how you want it, what would your life look like?" This question and questions like it assist helpers in seeing where clients want to go. It accepts the assumption that in therapy knowing where to go makes getting there much easier.

The solution-focused helper also looks for *exceptions* in the client's story. Exceptions are those components in clients' stories that do not fit for the problem they are sharing. For example, Kim worked with a client who knew she was a therapist and professor. He stated, "I have little empathy and want to change that." One day in session when he knew finals week was quickly approaching, he stated, "I bet this is a tough time of the semester for you." Kim smiled, and pointed out his empathetic statement, as an exception to his story.

Additionally, helpers look for and help clients find personal strengths. This *strength assessment* is vital, because it helps clients see their own resources that they can include in the process of change. This process of empowerment helps clients focus on their goals and their abilities and resources that can aid in achieving individual goals.

The solution-focused brief helper first attempts to build a therapeutic relationship. If successful, the therapist can move immediately to helping clients see what they want to change and how life can be different. Then, armed with techniques, the therapist helps the client gain insight and move to action. Therapy focuses not on the briefness of therapy but the immediate alleviation of those problems the client faces.

CHAPTER FIVE

CASE EXAMPLES FOR INTEGRATING THEORY TO PRACTICE

You cannot acquire experience by making experiments. You cannot create experience. You must undergo it.

—Albert Camus

As you search to integrate theory into your practice, you might wonder how others have worked through the Intentional Theory Selection [ITS] model of making theory practical. This chapter will provide you with several scenarios where the model can be used. The case studies included in the chapter represent (1) clinicians who have used the model to determine their theoretical orientation, (2) client cases where you will be able to apply the model to shape your theory and plan the helping relationship, and (3) supervision examples where you can apply the model to clinicians seeking supervision from you.

CLINICIAN CASE STUDIES

Now that you have perused the ITS model of making theory practical, you may choose to work through the process for yourself. A cursory reading of most theories textbooks can help you determine the theories you like best. However, the difficulty for most people occurs when the theory needs to be applied to a client sitting in front of them. This chapter will provide you with the experiences and reflections of four helpers as they worked through the ITS model of selecting a theoretical orientation. Each case is a real account of people in the helping professions who have utilized the ITS model. The helping professionals presented in the cases are diverse in their cultural backgrounds, field of study, practice settings, and years of experience in the field. Their experiences searching for a theoretical orientation are just as diverse and interesting. After each case study, reflection questions help you better understand the process of developing and solidifying your theoretical orientation.

Case One: Tony

Life Philosophy.   Prior to coming to my master's program, I had never really been "forced" to think about or verbalize my life philosophy. I had been through college, obtained a bachelor's degree in Family Services, and come out of that program still not knowing who I really was and what I wanted out of life. I'm not sure at that time I even wanted to figure these things out. I felt as if I was just "doing what I was supposed to do." I knew I had been through a lot since beginning college: many negative experiences with sex and relationships, alcohol and drug abuse, an abusive relationship, whittling relationships with friends and family, and many other things I struggled with through my first two years of college. When I came to this program, I was asked things I had never before been asked, and I had never asked myself. I had thought about them sporadically but had never been expected to answer them verbally or in written form. I was asked to define values and morals in general, and I remember this being difficult to do. To take steps further, I was expected to define my own specific personal values, morals, beliefs, and ideas about how the world works. After having gone through the first two years of my three-year program, I had a pretty good idea of what my own specific values, morals, and beliefs were as well as ideas about how the world works.

I think one of the most transforming and difficult processes for me was videotaping and having others view my videotapes and give feedback on my clinical skills. Learning to accept and positively view constructive criticism and feedback is the part of the process that helped me to partially figure out my life philosophy. I remember being crushed and feeling as if I was almost worthless after receiving feedback on my skills for the first few semesters. Now, I try to view the feedback as a necessary stepping-stone to get to where I am today. I now recognize that I needed to go through feeling crushed and almost worthless initially in order to want and appreciate all types of feedback. This process assisted me in defining what things I believe in, how I am, and the type of person I strive to be.

Participating in personal counseling is another factor that aided me in my transformation. My academic program required that I participate in a minimum of five sessions of personal counseling. I wanted to fulfill this requirement, but I also knew deep down inside that I truly needed to get some help. Areas of my life felt out of control, and I felt like I was sinking. Over a period of two years, I journeyed through the experience of counseling as a client. This process assisted me in defining who I am, my beliefs, and values. It also greatly helped me to understand how counseling really works. I believe I was partially exposed to a successful counselor-client relationship. I was able to learn the other side of the counselor-client relationship. I experienced the full range of the relationship from building trust to confrontation to termination. I now truly believe that one does not know how scary, stressful, terrifying, and uncomfortable counseling is for the client. I also now believe that unless one has been a client, one does not know how rewarding and fulfilling counseling can be for the client when they have the motivation to change. Throughout this process, I "found" myself and came to believe in myself, thus clarifying my beliefs, morals values, ideas of how the world works, and my life philosophy.

School of Thought.   In order to figure out my school of thought, I first needed to figure out my life philosophy. My own philosophy included my beliefs, morals, values, ideas of how the world works, self-understanding, and what gives meaning to my life. After I had figured out my life philosophy, I then began reading about the different schools of thought and deciding which ones fit my way of viewing the world and how I think it works. I tried to simultaneously figure out my life philosophy and into which school of thought it fit. I seemed to really struggle through this process, but it seemed to work out in the end. For the most part, I feel I have now figured it out. As I am nearing the completion of my master's degree, I realize that I have had ample opportunity for introspection.

Theory.   I have been able to feel grounded in selecting a theoretical orientation after reading books, taking additional courses, and completing my practical courses where I gained more experience with clients. I wanted to pick a theory and then try to use it with clients in addition to using the techniques with them. This felt so uncomfortable to me, almost as if I wasn't myself in session. It was very frustrating and anxiety provoking because that's how I thought the theory should work and it didn't. I felt like the process was so ambiguous and didn't understand why it had to be "backwards". "Trust the process" is what I have continued to hear from professors and have continued to tell myself. What I found was I needed to have experience being myself with clients and not focusing on what theoretical orientation I was using in sessions. I found that using my own personality and then fitting that style into a theory or theories, really worked for me.

Techniques and Goals.   I have a base of general techniques and goals I use with each client but other ones are developed or matched after I have developed a therapeutic relationship with my client. I base techniques on the client's personality and what I think they will most accept. I may use techniques more directly or I will use them more collaboratively with the client. It just seems to depend on the person. The way I figured out that this works best with me was to experiment in sessions with different ideas and techniques. That seemed to be the best way for me to practically find out what seemed to fit.

REFLECTION QUESTIONS

After reading Tony's experience, answer the following questions.

1. What did you learn from Tony's process?

2. What were the key moments in Tony's learning?

3. When were major transitions in Tony's development as a professional helper?

4. What were your thoughts and feelings as your read Tony's journey?

5. With which aspects of Tony's development can you identify?

6. Which parts of Tony's story are more difficult for you to identify?

Case Two: Jill

Life Philosophy.   As I have gone through the first building block in making theory practical, I have realized that examining life philosophy is as complicated as it sounds. Asking questions such as "What is truth?" and "Are people good?" takes courage and motivation. I have found that I must look inside myself to answer these questions and that the answers are true only for me. My ultimate answer to life philosophy has been to realize that mine changes daily and no one else thinks, feels, or views the world in the same way. I find myself examining my life philosophy with each new client who sits in front of me, and it changes, expands, contracts, and shifts based on each new circumstance. I may ask the same questions in each situation, but the answers will inevitably be different. How would I react in this situation? What coping mechanisms would I employ? What are this person's coping mechanisms? Does this person have a support system? What are his or her resources? What are my expectations of this situation based on my unique worldview?

In examining these questions, I have come to the conclusion that I am a person who emphasizes thinking. It is my view that our actions influence our thoughts and vice versa. Clients may present with distortions of thought, may act before thinking, or be able to think but not act. Understanding that I place importance on thinking has led me fluidly to the next building block, which is choosing a school of thought.

School of Thought.   In examining each school of thought, I have asked the questions "What is it about this school of thought that matches the way I think and feel about the world?" and "Are there components that I feel contradict my views?" In other words, what can I take from this school of thought and what can I discard? This is the tedious aspect of choosing theory in that it requires a lot of reading and research. I found myself looking first at the founders of the theory and then branching out to emerging theorists. What I found is that there are aspects of cognitive-behavioral theory that fit my personal style and aspects of humanistic theory, which I deem essential. Once chosen, I began to break down these schools of thought and begin to look at individual aspects of theory, which leads to choosing theory.

Theory.   Determining a person's theory is a delicate process that can become frustrating. When I first began looking at theory, I had the idea that I needed to agree with all the tenets in order to call it my chosen theory. Through instruction and discussion, I have found that choosing a theory is like choosing a piece of chocolate from a variety box. A person might choose a piece of chocolate, take a bite, find that he or she does not enjoy the taste, and put the piece back in the box or throw it away. Conversely, a person might choose a piece, take a bite, and find that piece of chocolate tastes wonderful on the tongue as well as stimulates the senses. Choosing aspects of theory can be similar in that a person might find an aspect that makes a light bulb appear above his or her head or choose a technique that inspires results consistently. As I began to look at cognitive-behavioral and humanistic theories, I found aspects that fit my personality such as the thinking-behavior connection, the essential component of building a solid therapeutic relationship, and the importance of providing education and opportunities for the client to practice therapeutic techniques outside of counseling sessions. Finally, choosing theory is not a linear process. A person chooses a theory or theories based on his or her worldview, which evolves over time. My worldview as a new clinician will not be the same as my worldview as a counseling professional with twenty years of experience. My professional and personal experiences will influence my worldview as well as my choice of theory throughout my life.

Goals and Techniques. Once a person chooses aspects of theory that fit his or her personality, it is easy to choose goals and techniques. I have chosen cognitive-behavioral and humanistic theories as my foundation. Therefore, my therapeutic goals most often center on assisting a person change behaviors, recognize irrational or unproductive thinking patterns, and process emotions surrounding life events. My techniques often involve providing education for the client, assigning and processing appropriate homework assignments with the client, and assisting the client in exploring emotions and thinking patterns. However, goals and techniques need to be flexible and a person needs to realize that he or she can choose techniques from all schools of thought. Different clients require different interventions, and counselors must be willing to look outside of their theory or theories to find suitable goals and techniques.

REFLECTION QUESTIONS

After reading Jill's experience, answer the following questions.

1. What did you learn from Jill's process?

2. What were the key moments in Jill's learning?

3. What were the major transitions in Jill's development as a professional helper?

4. What were your thoughts and feelings as your read Jill's journey?

5. With which aspects of Jill's development can you identify?

6. Which parts of Jill's story are more difficult for you to identify?

Case Three: Travis

I was excited to be able to participate in the workshop offered by the authors of this book because I wanted to find out which theoretical orientation would best fit my approach to counseling as I continue in my study to become a counseling psychologist. In my theories of psychotherapy class, we went through each theory and learned a variety of techniques. For my final project, I put a binder together, listing each theory, its theorist, and the techniques for each. But I was not satisfied. I did not know where to go from there. I knew that I preferred a few theories over others, but I did not know how to go about finding a theoretical orientation that would best fit. I brought my concern to the authors and had the opportunity to explore the Intentional Theory Selection model with them.

As I have gone through classes such as counseling skills and process with individuals, I feel that I have the knowledge and skills to counsel, but I just don't know how to put it towards a theoretical orientation. I am currently a therapist at a residential treatment facility, and I feel that a theoretical orientation would help me to guide my clients in a way that would be more beneficial. Some therapists, where I work, do not use theoretical orientation, but I feel it would help me be more consistent with my clients as I help guide them in the right direction.

The foundation of the ITS model is the life philosophy, what gives meaning to my life. As I sat down and pondered my life philosophy, I began to look back throughout my life and examined what has made me happy in the past. At times, when I am stressed out, I see myself sitting around talking with my family or being with my girlfriend. As I look back, what gives meaning to my life is my family and friends and being able to be there for one another. When I was a junior in college, my best friend from high school was in an accident and spent a couple of weeks in intensive care before he passed away. When something tragic happens, it makes you look at how you are living your life. What sets you apart from others? How you have been treating others? Where do you want to go? How much time do you have left to achieve your goals? Who do you want there, standing at the finish line, supporting you as you accomplish a major task? When I sit down and think about my life philosophy, that is what I think gives meaning to my life. As I took the Selective Theory Sorter, it really helped me put things into perspective. The questions are not questions that an individual would think about on a day-to-day basis. When answering the questions, I needed to sit down and think about them. When I received my results, it stated that I believed thoughts lead to actions and misconceptions lead to problems. I see that a lot with the clients I am working with now. When a client that I am working with has a misconception, he or she will continue to view that misconception until he or she thinks about it in a different way. I also did the values exercise from Chapter 3. From this I found I would like more peace, balance, serenity, and quality time with others. It is hard to be free from stress and emotion while going to graduate school, working 30–35 hours per week, finding time to do homework and study, yet spending time with the people I love. Being able to spend time with my family and friends means a lot to me. My family has always supported me and spending time with my family helps me achieve more balance and serenity. The results also indicated that in myself I value: motivation, being supported, being driven, perseverance, accomplishment, balance, and even temper.

Examining my values and life philosophy helped me put things into perspective. I started thinking back a couple years how I never would leave any time throughout my day to sit down and watch a half hour television program or read a magazine without feeling guilty about wasting some time. I have learned to slow down and to take a half hour break or call up an old friend or family member. I feel better when I am doing things that are important to me as they give more meaning to my life. Understanding the world around us is a necessity as we look at our life philosophy, especially since mental health counselors are working with individuals on a day-to-day basis. How a person thinks largely determines how one feels and behaves. I also think it is important to see what gives meaning to a client's life and what motivates them.

The next step is examining the schools of thought. I think I have a pretty good grasp on the schools of thought from my academic program. As I review the five schools of thought, the most appealing to me are the behavioral and pragmatic approaches. I feel that psychodynamic does not fit my thoughts or beliefs. I think I would have a hard time having a psychodynamic approach in my counseling mostly because I do not believe in a lot of the psychoanalytic views. Behavioral theory is appealing to me because I feel that humans are shaped and determined by sociocultural conditioning and learn through conditioning and reinforcement. I also like cognitive-behavioral theory because I believe that a change in one's cognition will result in changes in the individual's behaviors and actions.

I felt that taking the Selective Theory Sorter would be most beneficial to picking my own theory because it would help me determine how I view the theories. When I received my results back, it stated that I lean greatly towards the pragmatic schools of thought, having values with CBT, REBT, and reality therapy. These all require examination of cognitions as well as examining client wants and needs. The top three statements that I ascribed to were: (1) How a person thinks largely determines how one feels and behaves, (2) irrational beliefs are the principal of emotional disturbance, and (3) recognizing cognitive processing in emotion and behavior is central in therapy. These results were extremely helpful in putting my views into a theoretical orientation.

As I narrowed down my schools of thought and specific theories of interest, I thought about goals and techniques I would use. I will ultimately choose goals and techniques based on my theoretical orientation. I think finding the different techniques will be easy to explore now that I have a general idea of what theoretical orientation fits my values and beliefs.

As I read the first two chapters of this book and explored the ITS model, I felt more confident in my theoretical orientation. I feel that the ITS model is beneficial with tying up the loose ends to my theories class. In order to understand what theory I liked best and which one would fit my values and beliefs as I counsel, the ITS model helped guide me in the right direction. I think taking the time and effort to understand and walk through the steps of the model is very beneficial. The starting point really needs to be life philosophy, how you view yourself, others around you, and the world. If your theoretical orientation does not fit your views, then it is not going to work for you or your client. I think having the life philosophy, as the first step is a good choice. I like how the ITS model breaks down the school of thought and keeps it separate from the individual theories. It helped me to go through and look at the five different schools of thought before I took a look at all of the individual theories. It was not as overwhelming. Also, having the techniques and goals is a good feature to have at the ends of the ITS model. If you only picked your theory but did not research the techniques and goals to go with it, you would only have a theory but no way to guide your client. The ITS model helps you walk your way through figuring out your theoretical orientation in an easy and accurate way.

REFLECTION QUESTIONS

After reading Travis's experience, answer the following questions.

1. What did you learn from Travis's process?

2. What were the key moments in Travis's learning?

3. What were the major transitions in Travis's development as a professional helper?

4. What were your thoughts and feelings as your read Travis's journey?

5. With which aspects of Travis's development can you identify?

6. Which parts of Travis's story are more difficult for you to identify?

Case Four: Ryan

This counselor decided that going through the ITS model of making theory practical would be best accomplished by putting his thoughts into a song. The song is sung to the tune of the theme to the Beverly Hillbillies and goes like this:

> Let me tell you bout a man named Ry,
> Poor grad student, barely getting by.
> Lookin' at himself, cause he doesn't have a wife
> He saw a philosophical way of lookin' at his life
> Existentialism, that is, humanism.
> Well the next thing you know ol' Ry's a counseling fool
> Found his theory, readin' books, now he's feeling pretty cool.
> Advice and directions other counselors are givin'
> Old Ryan says "everyone's dying, only some of us are livin"
> Self-discovery that is, meaning, searching.
> Life's getting better and things are lookin' up
> To help find himself, Ryan thought he'd get himself a little pup.
> Ryan's ex-girlfriends he won't be takin' back,
> Cause he's found a friend that doesn't talk back.
> Lickin' faces, waggin' tails, unconditional love.
> As we say goodbye, there's one more thing we need to know.
> Winter is a comin', and we'll soon be playin' in the snow.
> If the weather has you down while you're gazing at it snowing,
> Remember Ryan's here to talk about where you've been and where you're going.
> Good listener he is, walks in your shoes,
> Phenomenological.

Comment on the Cases

Each of the helpers described their experiences working through the ITS model. Since each of them approached the ITS model in different ways, each had unique results and experiences. Tony's experience reflects that of a new helping professional who has struggled a great deal with his own emotional growth during his educational process of becoming a helping professional. Jill's experience reflects a person confident in her theoretical orientation and ways of viewing the world. Travis's experience shows that of a counselor who experienced death of someone close to him and left the situation with clearer priorities for his life. Ryan's experience reflects both introspection and creativity. Though his ITS model is not examined in the same way as the other three, he has clearly thought about and articulated his theoretical orientation.

Now that you have had a chance to see how other helpers have used the ITS model, you will have the opportunity to read about ways the model can be used in both clinical and supervision situations. The model is valuable not only in determining your own theoretical orientation, but it can also help you to work with clients. The following clinical cases are representative of clients you may see in your work as a helping professional. After each case is presented, you will have the opportunity to respond to the reflection questions that follow.

CLIENT CASE STUDIES

Case One: Tim

Tim is a 28-year-old, African-American male who lives alone and attends graduate school on a part-time basis. He supports himself by working as a stock clerk in a local department store. He completed his coursework for a master's degree in human resources four years ago, but he has yet to begin the thesis needed to earn the degree. Tim presents with flat affect and reports being unhappy most of his life. He reports that his father had a history with drug use and that his mother died of a cocaine overdose when he was 12 years old. Tim reports no history of drug or alcohol use. He is seeking counseling to deal with his relationships with women. His current relationship is the longest he has ever sustained. He states that girlfriends find him "too clingy" and it appears that his current girlfriend of eight months is also frustrated by his neediness. Tim wants to make this relationship work. He feels that his girlfriend is "the one" and wants your help learning new ways to be "less clingy."

REFLECTION QUESTIONS

1. What concerns do you have about working with Tim?

2. How does your life philosophy affect your view of Tim?

3. Which of your personal values might affect your work with Tim?

4. What, if any, cultural factors might play a role in your relationship with Tim?

5. Which theory or theories parallel your values and views?

6. What goals will you set in your work with this client?

7. Which techniques will you use?

Case Two: Barbara

Barbara is a 35-year-old, Caucasian woman seeking treatment to determine "what to do about my marriage." Barbara has been married for 13 years and has engaged in "a couple other relationships" since the second year of her marriage. Barbara reports that her husband is "nice but annoys me." Barbara states that she has stayed in her marriage because people would think she is an idiot to leave a guy as great as her husband. Barbara states that one of her extramarital relationships has gone on for eleven years. She believes this extra-marital relationship is "exactly what" she really wants. However, she feels stuck. Barbara wants your help making this "huge" decision about her marriage.

REFLECTION QUESTIONS

1. What concerns do you have about working with Barbara?

2. How does your life philosophy affect your view of Barbara?

3. Which of your personal values might affect your work with Barbara?

4. What, if any, cultural factors might play a role in your relationship with Barbara?

5. Which theory or theories parallel your values and views?

6. What goals will you set in your work with this client?

7. Which techniques will you use?

Case Three: Cheryl

Cheryl is a 19-year-old, college sophomore. She is seeking counseling to deal with three issues: (1) feelings of depression, (2) her tendencies toward perfectionism, and (3) her fear of feeling attracted to women. In your work with Cheryl, she determines that she needs medication for her depression. A doctor at the student health clinic gives her a prescription and she feels "a lot less depressed" within a month of beginning the medication. Cheryl continues coming to see you. In your work together, she realizes that her depression and perfectionism are due to her "romantic feelings towards women." Cheryl decides that she would like to focus her time with you on figuring out whether or not she is a lesbian. Specifically, she wants help figuring out how her feelings towards people of the same gender intersect with her Christian upbringing. Cheryl is also concerned about how her family members and friends may react to her *if* she is a lesbian.

REFLECTION QUESTIONS

1. What concerns do you have about working with Cheryl?

2. How does your life philosophy affect your view of Cheryl?

3. Which of your personal values might affect your work with Cheryl?

4. What, if any, cultural factors might play a role in your relationship with Cheryl?

5. Which theory or theories parallel your values and views?

6. What goals will you set in your work with this client?

7. Which techniques will you use?

SUPERVISORY CASE STUDIES

Now, you have experienced the Intentional Theory Selection [ITS] model as a tool with which to examine your theoretical orientation as well as some clinical cases. You will now have the opportunity to use the model in a supervision setting. Most clinicians in the helping professions have strong opinions regarding clinical supervision. Specifically, you may be familiar with the supervisory styles you like and do not like. You may be able to recall certain interventions and strategies that worked better for you than others. As you become a professional helper, you too, will likely have the opportunity to serve as a clinical supervisor, because professional helpers are often asked or required to supervise students and colleagues new to the profession. In your role as a supervisor, you may find the ITS model helpful to you. The following cases offer the chance to apply the model with those whom you will supervise.

Case One: Grace:

As a seasoned mental health counselor who works in a community agency, you have been asked to supervise a new mental health counselor named Grace. In your weekly supervision meetings, you notice how easily Grace engages you. She is very affective oriented. Her level of empathy and reflection of feeling are far greater than you would anticipate from someone with this level of experience. You perceive that Grace is humanistic oriented. Unfortunately, you are surprised when you watch the videotapes of her counseling sessions. In every session she tries to do behavior modification. She approaches each session, regardless of the client's issue, with a preset plan for behavior modification. You notice that Grace is so intent on behavior modification that she misses what the clients are saying.

REFLECTION QUESTIONS

Using the ITS model as a guide, answer the following questions:

1. How can you help Grace become more congruent?

2. How can you help this new professional pick a theory that is more congruent with whom she is as a person?

3. How would your own theoretical orientation hinder or help your work with this supervisee?

4. Where do you think Grace falls on the ITS model of making theory practical?

Case Two: Dominic

You are the director of a college counseling center and have taken on the supervision of a new, social-work intern named Dominic. He is eager to work with college students and believes he is an existentialist and "really open to feedback." In your supervision of Dominic, you are consistently impressed with his ability to build rapport with clients and construct meaning in their stories. He is caring and open to concerns that clients share with him. He tells you during a supervision meeting that he "really likes" one of his clients because of the growth she is attempting. When you watch the videotape, you notice that Dominic seems to be flirting more with the client than conducting therapy. You ask Dominic about his nonverbal communication with the client, and he states that he is "just concerned" about her. As you watched more of the tape, you noticed that Dominic does not utilize any counseling skills. When you confront Dominic on this, he says, "You must not have watched the whole tape!" He is enraged and unable to hear your concerns about his potential attraction to the client.

REFLECTION QUESTIONS

Using the ITS model as a guide, answer the following questions:

1. How can you help Dominic become more congruent between his stated theoretical orientation and his behavior on tape?

2. How can you help Dominic use his existential theory to understand what you see as countertransference?

3. How would your own theoretical orientation hinder or help your work with Dominic?

4. Which pieces of the ITS model of making theory practical would be most relevant for Dominic to revisit?

Case Three: Jason

You are working as the director for your city's hospice program and supervising Jason, a staff counselor with 10 years experience. Jason has worked at the hospice facility for three years and received excellent evaluations each year. Lately, you have heard from

Jason's clients that he seems less interested than he once did. Many clients have complained that Jason wants them to go to group therapy instead of seeing him so frequently as individual counseling clients. In your concern for Jason and the clients, you talk with him. During the course of the conversation, Jason shares with you that his way of looking at the world has changed. His wife is battling cancer, and Jason reports that they have greatly benefited from group therapy. He thinks group therapy is underutilized among people and families with cancer. He would like you to expand your view of his position so as to provide individual and group counseling. You want to be sensitive to Jason as a colleague and friend. However, his position is to provide individual counseling to the clients your office serves. Additionally, group counseling is provided under contract by another agency.

REFLECTION QUESTIONS

1. Which steps of the ITS model would you recommend Jason examine?

2. How can you help Jason to incorporate his values into his work?

3. What recommendations would you make to Jason to ensure he has sufficient support?

Summary

> But perhaps after this descent into yourself and into your inner solitude you will have to give up becoming a poet . . . But even then this inward searching which I ask of you will not have been in vain. Your life will in any case find its own ways thence, and that they may be good, rich and wide. . .
>
> —Rainer Maria Rilke

The Intentional Theory Selection (ITS) model can serve as both a practical and conceptual tool in the helping professions. In this chapter we have presented several applied ways the model can be utilized by students, professional helpers, and supervisors. As was clear in several of the case studies, in finding your theoretical orientation you may have challenges along the way. Additionally, when working with specific client populations, your specific theory and values may be challenged, because many clients will have a worldview that diverges from your own. As a future supervisor, you may also find yourself wanting to assist helpers as they develop and solidify their theoretical orientation.

Additionally, choosing a theory that is based on your personal life philosophy and values has an extra challenge, because life experiences will change your worldview. As shown in the case examples, transitions will likely challenge you in personal and professional endeavors. Life philosophy is the foundation of the ITS model. Consequently, as a developing professional, you may find that intermittently reviewing your own theoretical development is necessary and refreshing.

PUTTING IT ALL TOGETHER

Importance Revisited

Theoretical orientations in the helping professions serve many purposes. Accountability and intentionality are important aspects to the field of counseling, because actions and words may have huge impacts on the lives of clients. Research has driven the effectiveness of counseling theory, and consequently, helpers must provide techniques and interventions that have been proven to work. The only way helpers can do this is to be founded in theory. Legal mandates, ethical codes, and informed consent also require that helping professionals have a personal theoretical orientation and are able to articulate it.

Having a defined theory is important to the work of a counselor, because theory can serve as a roadmap to understanding the direction to take with clients. Additionally, when counselors need direction both during and outside of the therapy session, theory can serve as a conceptual tool aiding the counselor.

How Theory Is Found

Training programs often require students to articulate their theory of counseling. However, often students are given little support in how to choose a theory from which to work. Most students find their theory in one of three ways: They choose (1) the theoretical orientation of the helper's training program; (2) the helper's life philosophy; and/or (3) the helper's experience as a helper and/or a client (Hackney, 1992). However, these traditional methods each have their unique weaknesses.

Because of the need for a more comprehensive model of choosing a theory, the Intentional Theory Selection (ITS) model was developed. This model offers direction in finding a theory of counseling and finding a theory that is congruent with helpers' life philosophy and values.

This model is based on life philosophy. Through such processes as value clarification or the Selective Theory Sorter, counselors may explore their own beliefs and values. This exploration is the first step in finding a theoretical orientation that is congruent with the counselor's core beliefs. Once this objective is achieved, though difficult, counselors then look at the already existing body of knowledge to see what school of thought and theory best fits them. Luckily, research on effective therapies already exists, and counselors can pursue and digest the material already available.

Benefit of the ITS Model

The ITS model can serve several groups of individuals. First, it can provide direction for students seeking out their theories. However, as life experiences and transitions occur, professionals in the field, too, may seek to hone or change their theoretical orientation. Second, it can serve as a conceptual, clinical tool outside of the therapy hour.

Finally, the ITS model can help reach those professionals and students facing theoretical challenges.

The Field

The helping profession is a dynamic and ever-evolving field. Counselors, social workers, and psychologists all have a career that serves the public in important ways. Through prevention and therapy, these meaningful fields provide unique opportunities for both the public and the profession. As a profession, the helping field is constantly challenging the clients they serve. Thus professionals, as well, must accept being continuously challenged. Clients are constantly asked to seek, grow, and change. Counselors too have this same opportunity to change both as professionals and people.

REFERENCES

Adler, A. (1998). *What life could mean to you?* Center City, MN: Hazelden Information Education.

Adler, A., Ansbacher, H. L, & Ansbacher, R. R. (1989). *Individual psychology of Alfred Adler: A systematic presentation in selections from his writings.* New York: HarperCollins.

Beck, A. T. (1976). *Cognitive therapy and the emotional disorders.* New York: International Universities Press.

Beck, A. T (1991). Cognitive therapy: A 30-year retrospective. *American Psychologist, 46,* 368–375.

Berg, K. B. (2003). *Children's solution work.* New York: W. W. Norton.

Consoli, A. J., & Williams (1999). The shared culture of counselors. *Counseling & Values 43* (2), 106–115.

Corey, G. (2004). *Theory and practice of counseling and psychotherapy,* (5th ed.). Pacific Grove, CA: Wadsworth.

Corsini, R. J. (1979). *Current psychotherapies* (2nd ed.). Itasca, IL: F. E. Peacock Publishers.

Day, S. X. (2004). *Theory and design in counseling and psychotherapy.* Boston: Houghton Mifflin.

de Shazer, S. (1985). *Keys to solution in brief therapy.* New York: W. W. Norton.

Doyle, R. E. (1998). *Essential skills and strategies in the helping process.* Pacific Grove, CA: Brooks-Cole.

Ellis, A. (1962). *A reason and emotion in psychohotherapy.* New York: Lyle Stuart.

Enns, C. Z. (1993). Twenty years of feminist counseling and therapy: From naming biases to implementing multifaceted practice. *The Counseling Psychologist, 21* (1), 3–87.

Frankl, V. (1967). *Psychotherapy and existentialism: Selected papers on Logotherapy.* New York: Washington Square Press.

Gilliland, B. E. & James R. K. (1998). *Theories and strategies in counseling and psychotherapy.* Boston: Allyn & Bacon.

Glasser, W. (1965). *Reality therapy: A new approach to psychiatry.* New York: Guilford.

Glasser, W. (1998). *Choice theory: A new psychology of personal freedom.* New York: Harper-Perennial.

Hackney, H. (1992). Differentiating between counseling theory and process. *ERIC Digest,* ED347485.

Halbur, D. A. (2000). A *Q-methodological study of group members' experience of existential aspects of a training group.* Unpublished dissertation, University of South Dakota.

Hansen, J. C., Rossberg, R. K., & Cramer, S. H. (1993). *Counseling: Theory and process* (5th ed.). Boston: Allyn & Bacon.

Hansen, N. E. & Freimuth, M. (1997). Piecing the puzzle together: A model for understanding the theory-practice relationship. *The Counseling Psychologist 25* (4), 654–673.

Harris, T. A. (1969). *I'm OK-You're OK.* New York: Harper & Row.

Hazler, R. J. (2003). Person-centered theory in D. Capuzzi & D. R. Gross (Eds.), *Counseling and psychotherapy: Theories and interventions* (3rd ed.). pp. 157–180. Upper Saddle River, NJ: Merrill Prentice-Hall.

Ivey, A. E., D'Andrea, M., Ivey, M. B., & Simek-Morgan, L. (2002). *Theories of counseling and psychotherapy: A multicultural perspective.* Boston: Allyn & Bacon.

Ivey, A. E., & Ivey, M. B. (1999). *Intentional interviewing and counseling: Facilitating client development in a multicultural society.* Pacific Grove, CA: Wadsworth.

Ivey, A. E., Ivey, M. B., & Simek-Downing, L. (1987). *Counseling and psychotherapy: Integrating skills, theory, and practice.* Englewood Cliffs, NJ: Prentice-Hall.

Ivey, A., Ivey, M. B., and Simek-Morgan, L. (1997). *Counseling and psychotherapy: A multicultural perspective (4th e*d.). Boston: Allyn & Bacon.

Jackson, M., & Thompson, C. L. (1971) Effective Counselors: Characteristics and attitudes. *Journal of Counseling Psychology, 18* (3), 249–254.

Jongsma, A. E., & Peterson, L. M. (1995). *The complete adult psychotherapy treatment planner.* New York: John Wiley and Sons.

Jung, C. G. (1991). *The development of personality: Papers on child psychology, education and related subjects* (5th ed.). Translated by R. F. C. Hull. Edited by H. Head, M. Fordham, G. Ader, & W. McGuire. New York: Princeton University Press.

Kaufman, Y. (1979). Analytical psychotherapy. In Corsini, R. J. (Ed.), *Current Psychotherapies* (pp. 95–130). Itasca, IL: F. E. Peacock.

Kelly, G. (1955). *The psychology of personal constructs* (Vols. 1 and 2). New York: W. W. Norton.

Kottler, J. A. (1999). *The nuts & bolts of helping.* Boston: Allyn & Bacon.

Kottler, J. A. & Brown, R. W. (1992). *Introduction to therapeutic counseling* (2nd ed.). Pacific Grove, CA: Peacock.

Mancoske, R. J., Standifer, D., & Cauley, C. (1994). The effectiveness of brief counseling services for battered women. *Research on Social Work Practice, 4* (1), 53–56.

Mahalik, J. R. (1995). Practitioners' value orientation: Examination of core values and influence of theoretical orientation. *Counseling and Values 39* (3), 228–238.

Mahoney, M. (1991) *Human change processes: The scientific foundations of psychotherapy.* New York: Basic Books.

Mosak, H. H. (1979). Adlerian psychotherapy in R. J. Corsini's (Ed.), *Current Psychotherapy* (2nd ed.). pp. 44–94. Itasca, IL: F. E. Peacock.

Myers, I. B., & McCaulley, M.H. (1985). *Manual: A guide to the development and use of the Myers-Briggs Type Indicator.* Palo Alto, CA: Consulting Psychologists Press.

Myers, I. B., & McCaulley, M. H. (1998). *Manual: A guide to the development and use of the Myers-Buggs Type Indicator.* Palo Alto, CA: Consulting Psychologists Press.

Myers, P. B. & Myers, K. D. (1977). *Myers-Briggs Type Indicator, Form G.* Palo Alto, CA: Consulting Psychologists Press.

Nelson-Jones, R. (2000). *Six key approaches to counseling and therapy.* New York: Continuum.

Nichols, M. P., & Schwartz, R. C. (2001). *Family therapy: Concept and method* (5th ed.). Boston: Allyn & Bacon.

Pedersen, P. B., Draguns, J. G., Lonner, W. J., & Trimble, J. E. (Eds.). (1996). *Counseling across cultures.* Thousand Oaks, CA: Sage.

Pedersen, P. B., & Ivey, A. E. (1993). *Culture-centered counseling and interviewing skills: A practical guide.* Westport, CT: Praeger.

Perls, F. S. (1969a). *In and out of the garbage pail.* Moab, UT: Real People's Press.

Perls, F. S. (1969b). *Gestalt therapy verbatium.* Moab, Utah: Real People Press.

Poznanski, J. J., & McLennan, J. (1995). Conceptualizing and measuring counselors' theoretical orientation. *Journal of Counseling Psychology, 42* (4), 411–422.

Rogers, C. (1957). The necessary and sufficient conditions of therapeutic personality change. *Journal of Consulting Psychology, 21*, 95–103.

Rogers, C. (1961). *On becoming a person.* Boston: Houghton-Mifflin.

Rogers, C. (1995). *On becoming a person: A therapist's view of psychotherapy.* Boston: Houghton Mifflin.

Rosen, H., & Kuehlwein, K. T. (1996). *Constructing realities: Meaning-making perspectives for psychotherapist.* San Francisco: Jossey-Bass.

Srebalus, D. & Brown, D. (2001). A *Guide to the helping professions*. Boston: Allyn & Bacon.

Strohmer, D. V., Shivy, V. A., & Chodo, A. L. (1990). Information processing strategies in counselor hypotheses testing: The role of selective memory and expectancy. *Journal of Counseling Psychology 37* (4), 465–472.

Strupp, H. H. (1955). An objective comparison of Rogerian and psychoanalytic techniques. *Journal of Consulting Psychology, 19*, 1–7.

Sue, D. W., & Sue, D. (2003). *Counseling the culturally diverse: Theory and practive* (4th ed.). New York: John Wiley & Sons.

Watts, R. (1993). Developing a personal theory of counseling: A brief guide for students. *TCA Journal, 21* (1), 103–104.

Weist, D. J., Wong, E. H., Brotherton, S., & Cervantes, J. M. (2001). Postmodern counseling: Using narrative approaches in the school setting. *Family Therapy, 28* (1), 1–17.

Willis, C. T. (1989). The Myers-Briggs Type Indicator. *Test Critiques* (Volume 10). Buros Bureau of Mental Measurements.

Yalom, I. (1995). *Group psychotherapy*. New York: Basic Books.

Young, M. E. (1998). *Learning the art of helping*. Upper Saddle River, NJ: Prentice Hall

Zimmerman, J. L., & Dickerson, V. C. (1996). *If problems talked: Narrative therapy in action*. New York: Guilford.

INDEX

Note: Information presented in tables and figures is denoted by *t* or *f* respectively.